My Life *as a* Caregiver

HOW I BECAME THE BEST IN THE FIELD

VOLUME 3

ANTONETTE SMITH

PAGE PUBLISHING, INC.
New York, NY

First originally published by Page Publishing, Inc. 2019

ISBN 978-1-64544-586-9 (Paperback)
ISBN 978-1-64544-587-6 (Digital)

Printed in the United States of America

DEDICATION

I would like to thank all the people that God sent into my life that helped and trained me into the woman I am today. God created my life from my end to my beginning. It is he that chose to birth me into this earth realm in 1976. It is he that chose my parents and the situation or circumstances that surrounded my conception, birth, and upbringing. It is he that chose the different tutors, teachers, preachers to help govern my life. I thank my Father Jehovah for being my Creator and Master. I thank my Lord Jesus for his life to redeem me and restore me back to our Father. I thank the Holy Spirit who is the Spirit of Truth that takes me into the deep things of God.

In this third book of the *Behind the Scenes* series, I will honor the people that had the greatest impact in my life that trained me into becoming a caregiver and to be the best in my field. I would not have been who I am today had it not been for these precious people God ordained, trained, and placed into my life. I am eternally grateful and thankful to them all. Sit back, relax, get a bowl of popcorn, and read my life as a caregiver and how I became the best in my field.

CONTENTS

Chapters

CHAPTER 1

GIVEN PURPOSE

Who then is Paul, and who is Apollos, but ministers by whom ye believed, even as the Lord gave to every man? I have planted, Apollos watered; but God gave the increase. So then neither is he that planteth and he that watereth; but God that giveth the increase. Now he that planeth and he that watereth are one: every man shall receive his own reward according to his own labour. For we are labourers together with God; ye are God's husbandry, ye are God's building. According to the grace of God given unto me, as a wise master-builder, I have laid the foundation, and another buildeth thereon. But let every man take heed how he buildeth thereupon. For other foundation can no man lay than is laid, which is Jesus Christ. Now if any man build upon this foundation gold, silver, precious stones, wood, hay, stubble; every man's work shall be made manifest: for the day shall declare it, because it shall be revealed by fire; and the fire shall try every man's work of what sort it is. If any man's work abide which he hath built thereupon, he shall receive a reward. If any man's work shall be burned, he shall suffer loss: but he himself shall be saved; yet so as by fire.

—First Corinthians 3:5–15, KJV

The summer at age five was a twofold summer, to say the least. The beginning of the summer was when the molestation started in my life that altered the very course of my life, I *thought*. But God knew my end from my beginning. The end of this same summer, my life was given purpose.

My father, the late Jentle Pendleton "Big Jim" as they called him. I called him Jim because I was raised calling my stepfather daddy. Like I heard, my brothers call him Jim.

It wasn't until I was nine years old I found out he was my biological father. Now he has always been in my life, taking care of me, picking me up, keeping me, calling me his baby. Those were his favorite words "*my baby*" this and "*my baby*" that. He and my mother just assumed I knew he was my biological father because they both would say, "your daddy."

But my mom said the same thing about my stepfather when he came to pick us up for the weekend, holidays, and summer. But my father, Jim, would always bring me to Wesson, Mississippi, two to three times a year, sometimes more, it just depends what is taking place. Now my father would bring me regularly because his mother, sister, and three brothers still lived in Mississippi. My aunt and uncle raised me from age four to six weeks until I was almost three years old. I still don't know the story behind that, but there I was. Now when I was born, my father was fifty-two years old, my grandmother his mother was seventy-six years old, and my aunt that raised me was fifty-four years at the time of my birth. At age five, my father and aunt began to train me in caring for my grandmother. She was a new diabetic and required insulin shots and bathing. I first began combing and scratching all three of their heads in one day. They took turns.

I started with my grandmother. I still remember the smell of her hair and grease we used. My grandmother was mixed with Indian. She had curly hair. You apply grease to it, and it curls up. She loved for you to scratch in the top of her head. She had some type of birthmark I used to mess with all the time.

But she would fall asleep as I scratched her head. If I would begin to stop, she would wake up and say, "Scratch right here, Anjonette." LOL. She pronounced my name with a J instead of T. My head-scratching would last about twenty to thirty minutes, greasing her scalp and learning to braid with plaiting hair as they called it in Mississippi. Then my aunt would say, "Come scratch my head. Oh, how it itches me so bad." Now my aunt had good hair too. She wore a carefree curl and loved to dig in her head and apply Care Free Moisturizer to her scalp.

She too would allow me to practice braiding and plaiting her hair for twenty to thirty minutes. Each time I thought I was done, she would say, "Scratch right here."

I was very impatient and wanted to go play. I didn't want to comb hair, scratch heads, or be in the house. And to top it all off, just whose head is next? That's right—my father. Now my father was already a trip. He would have me lay on his chest and pluck the hairs out of his face with tweezers as early as I can remember, and it was before this summer.

He told me as a baby I loved to climb on his chest and play with the hair on his face. I would laugh each time he told me that story because my aunt said I did my uncle the same way. I loved to be on their chest in their face. I am still that way today as an adult. When I was married or in any sexual relationship, I always loved to lay on my man's chest and play in his face. I really just love to watch him as he talks. He has my undivided attention. You can thank my father and uncle for that behavior and character of grace and truth. I truly believe in giving my male counterpart my undivided attention by just focusing on them. I think well I knew they need that time to connect, one on one. Because let's face it, women, during the day and the night, we're worrying and focusing on the children, the house, the job, the family, our grocery list, our hair, our nails, our friends, and when the man needed us, we wear out and tired and have nothing left for them. So this is one of the greatest gifts and purposes my father, my uncle, my grandmother, and my aunt gave to me—how to be a caregiver.

Being a caregiver is defined in many ways.

Caregiver—a family member or paid helper who regularly looks after a child or a sick, elderly, or disabled person. A person who provide direct care to children, elderly, sick, or disabled persons.

Caregivers are typically professionals, home health aides, personal care aides, nursing assistants, in-home companions or family members or friends who provide vital physical, practical, and emotional support to a person who is elderly, disabled, or senior.

So you see the variety of duties and roles a caregiver could perform. So my father knew that I was very, very, very impatient. He used to make me pick his face for hours. He would fall asleep. Just like my grandmother and aunt as I scratched his head and woke up, he would say, "Scratch right here, baby." Now that I think about it, he always looked at his watch when he woke up; maybe he was timing me. He used to make me sit at the table and play cards for hours because he said I needed to learn to sit still and stop running around and act like a little girl. Well, I was a tomboy to the fullest. I climbed trees, played football, baseball, and basketball, jumped off the roof several times.

Whatever my brothers did, I did too. I was the only girl with three brothers and the baby I had to keep up with them.

Now that I have learned how to scratch heads like a professional and pick facial hairs with tweezers and have a little more patience, I will increase in learning. Now at age seven, I was assigned to help my grandmother take her bath. Now she fought me with tooth and nail because she declared she didn't need help bathing. She was eighty-three now. But my father said to help her, and I was instructed to obey my father, not my grandmother.

"She told me to get out of the bathroom," I told my father.

My aunt came into her bathroom and said, "Momma, let Tookie help you get your bath."

She argued, "I don't need no help."

My aunt looked at me and said, "Help Momma get her bath."

I said, "Yes, ma'am."

So I told my grandmother, "I will just wash your back, okay?"

Only God knows how I was able to think to tell my grandmother that. I said, "Just let me wash your back, Grandma."

I was thinking because I don't want to get fussed at by my father or my aunt, now either of them *never* whooped me for anything. I was spoiled rotten by them and my brothers, LOL. I know I was a little brat, but hey, I was the baby—their baby. To my father and them, I was a miracle child, a gift from God to them. And now I know why they felt that way because I now feel that way too. But they were giving me purpose under the guidance of the Holy Ghost. I was operating in an anointing given to me to be a caregiver.

Yes, I was anointed, but I had to be trained. You understand that? This is for all my anointed readers that say I am anointed to do this and that, but you also have to be trained to operate in that anointing and develop a character to balance your gifts. But that is a whole another book to write maybe the Father will tell me to write about it someday? We shall see.

So now that I assist my grandmother with bathing and dressing her, she said, "Thank you, Anjonette."

I dried her off, lotion her down, applied baby powder to her chest and dressed her in her duster, slip panties and house shoes that was her daily wardrobe. When we came out, Grandma was walking in front of me with her cane. My aunt and father had the biggest smile on their faces. I think they might have been at the door listening to us.

She said, "Time to eat."

I said, "Yes, ma'am."

I am hungry and tired. But my training was not done. My father said, "You need to watch Momma give herself her shot in case you have to give it to her."

I was like, "What?" I hate needles. I mean really hate them. When I had my third child, I took my baby to this clinic in our town and the same nurse was there from when I was a child. Now you got to remember I had my first child at age thirteen, second at fifteen, and third at sixteen. So the nurse wasn't old, I was just mature, LOL. So my baby needed his shots, and the nurse was about to give them.

She said to me, "I remember when you were in preschool."

And at the time, the school brought the school to the clinic to get shots each year.

She said, "I had given all the children their shots and looking for you, you were hiding. I said, 'Did you get your shots?' You said yes and got on the bus. I checked my paperwork and came and got you back off the bus. I brought you to my office to give you your shots, and you cried and screamed and fell on the floor like I was killing you. I had to get the other nurse to hold you down. We did this every year you came. Do you remember that? she said.

I said, "No, ma'am, but I hate shots."

She said, "Yes, since you were a child, you ran from needles, LOL."

We laughed, and she gave my son his shots, and each time I went, I heard the same story.

She would say, "I can't believe I gave you school shots. Now I'm giving your children school shots?"

So when my father told me to watch my grandmother, I almost fainted. I closed my eyes and frowned up. He said, "You can't see anything with your eyes closed."

I said, "I can't watch her. It hurts."

My grandmother said, "It doesn't hurt me, baby."

I said, "I will pass."

Well, they let me slide that day, but we were back at it the next morning, me watching for breakfast. My aunt got the insulin out of the refrigerator and the needle out the cabinet, alcohol pads, sugar machine, and meds box on the counter. I watched and followed her steps for breakfast. And by the way, my aunt wakes me up when she gets up. There is no sleeping in here. Get dressed, brush teeth, start laundry. Yes, you read it correctly—learning to wash clothes at age five.

You have to understand my aunt, grandmother, and father were all elderly, so someone had to be trained to care for them. It was myself and my cousin/brother Duke that was two years younger than me, and my aunt adopted him after my mother came and took me back to Illinois. He was my uncle's son, so we were cousins first. But we consider ourselves brother and sister because my aunt and uncle were our first parents to have us from birth. I think I was earlier when I came, but we both were weeks old. It wasn't that our fathers didn't love us because they absolutely did, but they wanted us to have a stable life and upbringing that my aunt and uncle could provide. So everything was about learning and living life.

To take care of yourself, your family, your parents they all were so bent and *huge* on family.

Because my grandmother had her first child at thirteen and birthed six children and gave them all away, my father and his siblings found each other and their mother, and they took care of each other.

My father was raised by his father, Amos, a Sioux Indian chief in Chicago. He said they moved to Chicago when he was sixteen years old, and he joined the Army. He fought in World War II. He lied about his age to get in the Army. My father loved this country, and so do I. I love servicemen and servicewomen. But my father or his sibling didn't hate my grandmother for giving them up. They loved her for giving them life and birthing them. He is where I get my heart of compassion from. Why be mad, angry, or unforgiving? Have mercy on people. It's hard to live in this world and make rightful decisions when you have everything against you. My grandmother was born on January 10, 1900, my father February 1, 1923, and my aunt April 5, 1921, all in Mississippi into slavery, so there you have it, you can fill in the blanks if you choose too.

Dinner—well, suppertime came, and I had to perform the duties at hand. I had to get my grandmother insulin out of the refrigerator, needle out the cabinet, alcohol pad and BS monitor, and medications off the counter. I had to thump the glass bottle of insulin to remove the air pockets, insert the needle, and draw insulin. I had to ask my grandmother where she wanted her shot because we had to rotate parts—stomach and front thigh.

She said, "You're giving me my shot?"

I said, "Yes, ma'am."

My aunt said, "She knows what she's doing, Momma. In case we're gone, you need your shot, Tookie can give it to you."

She said, "Okay, Anjonette, stick me in my legs, I guess."

I was so scared.

I was sweating and about to cry because I knew it hurt, and I was gonna pass smooth out on the floor. I looked at my aunt. I said, 'I can't do it."

She said, "Yes, you can."

My grandmother said, "Just stick me and hurry up."

I really got scared. I stuck her in the front thigh and gave her insulin shot, rubbed again with alcohol, and put the needle in the milk jug. They're both looking at me like "see, it wasn't that bad, was it?"

I said, "Yes, it was."

I wanted to vomit. I was so sick. I said, "Grandma, I am so sorry I hurt you."

She said, "You didn't hurt me, baby."

My grandmother, father, and aunt made me feel like I would do anything, and they took time out to train me, teach me, show me. They were older and settled down, so they were never in a hurry and didn't want me to be. They had patience in every area I think.

So they gave this little girl purpose and instilled a strong foundation of core values in me that would last me a lifetime. I had no idea what I had been given or imparted into me at this young and tender age. These are my roots—my grandmother, my father, and my aunt were my root system. They are where I get my foundational teaching skills from to teach, train, and mentor the children I work with. Lead them by example, not just in word but in deed also. You must train them early in life to set their foundation and course of their lives that they may be all God intended for them to be.

> Train up a child in the way he should go: and
> when he is old, he will not depart from it.
> —Proverbs 22:6, KJV

CHAPTER 2

SEEN PURPOSE

Age seven to eight

In this chapter, I will tell you how God began to allow others to see a purpose in me. I didn't have a clue what purpose was or what was taking place fully, but one thing was sure, God was looking down on me, and Jesus was with me and protecting me along with the host of angels.

No doubt in my mind, Jesus heard my daily prayers. It is so surreal because even in the midst of the episodes of molestation, I still maintained some sense of joy and happiness in myself. I was a happy child, always laughing and smiling. I was a serious child too. I took things to heart. If you told me something, I expected you to keep your word. That was my faith at work in me and the belief system of hope was taught at Bible Witness Camp. So this next story is where my faith was signed, sealed, and would deliver throughout my life. I told you in *The Real Antonette Come Forth* series that I was chosen to live a life of faith.

This is where my strong foundation of faith was built, imparted, and engrafted into me at a very early age. This is why I weathered the storms of my life quietly and why I totally depended on my Lord Jesus Christ then and now. I depend on Jesus to help me in any and every situation. No need to see a therapist—He is my counselor;

no need to talk about my problems—He is my solution; no need to worry about money—He is my provider. No need to wait for a superhero to rescue me—He is my Deliverer, and I understood all these things as a child.

That is why when I became pregnant at age thirteen, I didn't care what people said about me. I didn't care how they looked at me either. I didn't worry about how I was going to provide or care for my child. I already had provision made plain and in operation. In other words, I was already living by faith. I've already been persuaded that Jesus was my all in all. He had already proven Himself to me and answered many prayers for me. It would appear that He wasn't with me or hearing me when bad things would occur, but He was with me still, and He heard me still. I was operating in total faith with works in the vision and provision God had given me for my life. Many times I cried myself to sleep because it felt like Jesus wasn't with me. My circumstances looked as if He had left me many of times. But something inside me would not totally believe that, so I looked for him every day and in every way. You will read about my provision in chapter 6.

History of Bible Witness Camp

In the mid-1920s, God led Mrs. Jewel Pierpont to find Bible Witness Mission in Chicago, Illinois, after moving from San Francisco where an earthquake claimed the lives of her husband and only son. She suffered a nervous breakdown for many years. God took hold of her mind. When she relocated to Chicago, she saw hundreds of black children roaming the streets like sheep without a shepherd. That is when the Lord led her to her faithful sister Martha Seeberger to start Bible Witness Mission. Witnessing that the Bible is true from cover to cover and explains the only way to eternal salvation—faith in Jesus Christ.

From the beginning, the financial policy has been one of faith in God's provision without pleas for money or fund-raising methods. The work of George Mueller had impressed them both. They claimed Philippians 4:19 (KJV), "My God shall supply all your needs according to His riches and glory by Christ Jesus." For more than thirty years, the women witnessed God provide their needs. Bible Witness Camp is born in the 1940s. Mrs. Ford purchased a thirty-two-acre lot located in Pembroke Township, Kankakee County, Illinois, just sixty-five miles South of Chicago to hold ten-day summer camps for city children to enjoy the country. The first camp was in 1947, ten days for boys and ten days for girls. *No charge to the campers.* They "earned" the week through a program of scripture memory. Trudie Sylvester attended girls camp that first summer and returned next year to be a counselor in 1948. In 1949, she left for Trinidad to serve the Lord as a missionary. Each year, the scenery changed for the camp as more families from Chicago moved to Pembroke. Many southerners moved north to settle.

Mrs. Ford prayed to the Lord to send a family. She believed that if a family came with children, it would draw more children. God answered her prayers and sent Reverend Marshall and Lizetta Williams from Wayland, Michigan. Mrs. Ford stayed overnight at their home after completing a revival.

She asked them to help pray that God would send a family to live and take over Bible Witness Camp that it may become a full-time ministry. Later that year, the Lord worked the hearts of the Williams family through prayer and instruction from Mrs. Ford. The scripture Isaiah 6:8 (KJV) "Whom Shall I send? Who will go for us?" The Williams response was the rest of the verse, "Here am I, send me."

They answered God's call together. In late August 1955, the couple went to mission on south state street in Chicago and volunteered to serve at Bible Witness Camp. From her sickbed, Mrs. Ford made one requirement for their acceptance.

"You will agree to missions. One requirement, trust the Lord for all your needs."

"We will," they responded.

They did. They found God faithful. Mrs. Ford died the next day. As Reverend Marshall and Lizetta Williams pulled into the sandy acreage with their four children, their personal and household goods, a car, two hundred dollars, and a promise of fifteen dollars a month from friends, plus the promises of God. The mission closed a year or two later, and the property was purchased by the Illinois Institute of Technology. Bible Witness Camp became the sole survivor of Mrs. Ford's original work (Bible Witness Camp, 2019).

My story of Bible Witness Camp and history of Pembroke, Illinois, I am the ages of seven and eight. I still attend Bible Witness Camp Girls Awana in Pembroke, Illinois, or Hopkins Park, Illinois, a.k.a. "Hollyrock" on Wednesday's and church on Sundays. The bus would pick us up for church on Sundays, and the van on Wednesday all driven by volunteers.

The camp provided free transportation to church and camp over a thirty-five-mile radius, covering all of Pembroke, Momence, St. Anne, Kankakee, Bourbonnais, Aroma Park, and the State Line by Indiana. All these places were full of children living in poverty, destitute conditions. Now in 2003, the *Oprah Winfrey Show* did a story on Pembroke Township, Hopkins Park, Illinois. She said, "Can you believe in the twenty-first-century people are still living in poverty?" She and others deemed Pembroke worse than a third-world country because some places still didn't have running water or electricity. Of course, I became upset when I heard the story. I had just moved to Mississippi. She talked to a lot of people in Hopkins Park that blow things completely out of portion. Yes, we had challenges with modern technology but poverty beyond a third-world country, that was a bit extreme. Until I began to get all the drugs out my system and seek Christ more, I began to remember and think a lot about my childhood. Because that really upset me, I wasn't gonna let it go. But I missed my father so much after his death I would think about all the times we shared.

And we spent a lot of time delivering food, clothes to families houses in these cities. He paid a lot of people bills and gave them work. I recalled the truck—the meat man named George (Caucasian)—he would come from Indiana and sell meat off the back of his truck to all the families in these same towns. He sold meat for food stamps. Every house got meat on credit from George because they would run out of food before the month was out. So he wrote your name in a book and gave you credit until food stamp day. He would come every week, one day to cover these cities, the next day to cover the other cities. He knew when and how much food stamps and checks everyone received.

George fed a lot of children and provided starvation in the homes. But because I wasn't faced with poverty due to my father's profession and my mother' wit, I didn't consider Hopkins Park to be in poverty. We never lived in government housing or any kind, no section 8, low income, or was never homeless. We always had new clothes, shoes, toys the latest. Both my father's took care of us. They both served this country, so us children received checks from their service to our country.

They both had work ethics and worked, so it wasn't like we were poor. We never lacked, and we always helped the less fortunate. My mother cooked and fed everyone, gave our clothes away all the time, and housed many people. We always had someone living or staying the night from adults to children to families. So in my eyes, Oprah, CNN, ABC, World News all was wrong about my city where I was born and raised. So the Lord gave me this scripture:

> The day following Jesus would go forth into Galilee, and findeth Philip, and saith unto him, "Follow me." Now Philip findeth Nathanael, and saith unto him, "We have found him, of whom Moses in the law, and the prophets, did write, Jesus of Nazareth, the son of Joseph." And Nathanael said unto him, "Can there any good thing come out of Nazareth? Philip saith unto him, come and see." (John 1:43–46, KJV)

This was my response to Oprah and the news crew when I wrote my first book of *The Real Antonette Come Forth Book* series. I shipped her assistant a copy with a letter addressed to her, asking her to do a follow up on the story she wrote about Hopkins Park in 2003. Because a lot of us children made it out of Pembroke because of Bible Witness Camp. They were the glue that held and still holds Pembroke together. We became pilots in the US Army, Marines, fashion designers, social workers, semitruck company owners, singers, actress, writers, business owners, and much more. They never talked to the people that weathered the storms of Hopkins Park that were a part of the building of this village. My grandfather and uncle helped founded the village of Hopkins Park who was runaway slaves from Alabama.

The Williams family that relocated from Michigan to minister to poor black children to fulfill God's will for our lives. I just felt like and still feel like that they didn't show honor to my city or the people of my city because they came in and found everything that was wrong and out of order according to them instead of printing a balanced story of the good and bad of a city. This is why I take time in all my books and writing to show honor to all those that have helped to get me to where I am today.

They never have to ask me to tell of my gratitude for them. Many are shocked when I show them that I have honored them publicly. Look, whether people were positive or negative in your life, they played their part to help shape and mold you. Either to be what you are or to not be like them in life, ministry or work you decide, but it is all learning and training if you ask me. I learn from people failures as well as their success. That is my take on my hometown that I still love.

I gave you a brief history on Bible Witness Camp and Pembroke that you may better understand my biblical foundation and life in Christ that has been embedded into me since a child. I consider myself like Timothy. Apostle Paul told him 2 Timothy 3:15 (KJV), "And that from a child thou hast known the scriptures, which are able to make thee wise unto salvation through faith which is in Christ Jesus."

I finally have said enough Bible verses to attend summer overnight camp. This was a huge accomplishment for me because my home life wasn't always peaceful to study scriptures.

We were home during the week for school and with our fathers on the weekends. My brothers would help me study for Awana and my cousin on the bus to camp. The leaders really worked hard with us children because they wanted us to succeed in every area of our lives.

The goal in Awana has many folds and rewards. The main goal and purpose are to learn about Jesus Christ our Lord and Savior first and foremost. So they have this system that works for children, even adults. You must be five years old to attend Awana Camp—the boys go on Monday nights, and the girls go on Wednesday nights. You must purchase an Awana book and vest. The book contains the Holy Scriptures that the child must learn and verbally say aloud to one of the camp leaders, and they sign their signature on the line under the scripture. Each scripture you say and get signed off, you get a black colored in on the bulletin board designed for overnight summer camp.

You have to learn so many scriptures to attend one week of over camp. You have one year to complete maybe five hundred scriptures to qualify. I am not sure if it was that many or more, but it was a lot, and you could say them at church, on the bus, anywhere a leader could listen to you. We would be walking from building to building trying to say these scriptures to make it to the overnight camp. It was wonderful and a great goal to have. Not only would we make it to the overnight camp, but we received "shares," fake one-dollar bills for each scripture we learned, and at the end of Awana, we could go to the Sugar Shack to purchase candy, chips, drinks with our "shares" fake one-dollar bills. This was very exciting for us children. We had our own money and could buy what we wanted. And it motivated you to learn scriptures.

Even if you didn't make it to the overnight camp, you were able to buy a snack each week. The parents were supposed to help us children learn the scriptures that we might participate in all Awana had to offer us. Another great part of Awana was if you were an obedient child and learned your scriptures, you were chosen to go to the Awana Olympics. The Olympics was held in Bloomington, Illinois, about a two-hour drive from Pembroke, Illinois—that alone was a treat to many of the children. We competed with other children from other churches saying Bible verses. They had judges, ribbons, trophies, and all. They would either give us the book of the Bible with verse and chapter, and we had to quote the scripture, or they would give the scripture, and we had to quote the book, chapter, and verse.

We had a wonderful time. We received awards and stripes for our Awana vest as we reached new levels by completing Awana books. I am telling you I had a wonderful childhood. This was the joy of my life then and now. And one song I will never forget we sang it every Sunday, "I Have Decided to Follow Jesus." That song and revelation were embedded into us, and that's my foundation in Christ.

Martin Luther King Jr. (Speaker)

Now our God is an awesome God. Since I was threatened to shut up and keep quiet from by abusers, God had to give me a stronger reason to talk and express myself positively. So He made me very inquisitive and curious to the point I asked so many questions it drove my parents crazy. My mom would say, "Don't question me. Just do what I tell you." Or "Slow down. You talk to fast." I was in a hurry to say what I wanted to say before I was told to shut up. I talked so fast my mom would make repeat myself over and over until she felt I talked slow enough.

Of course, I was upset and frustrated too with her because now she's adding to the *slow-me-down* group like my father. He would say, "I didn't understand anything you just said" when I talked fast. And when I was mad, I talked even faster. Even now when I speak if my mom in the audience, she always looked at me and waved her hands to tell me to slow down. When I use to write, which I have always loved, she would tell me that my brain moves faster than my hands and my mouth and to reread what I write. I finally listen now at age forty-three, LOL. Hey, what can I say? I am a work in progress. God will perfect those things that concerned me, even my speech, my tone, and definitely my delivery.

I am in the second grade, and my teacher's name is Mrs. Salsbury. Black History month is coming up, and we must prepare and say a speech for the program. She chooses who we will quote or speak like. She chose Dr. Martin Luther King Jr. for me to speak "I Have a Dream" speech. Oh boy, I would not wait to get home to tell my mother.

"Guess who I am going to be at school?"

She said, "Who, Tookie?"

I said, "I am going to be Dr. Martin Luther King Jr. 'I Have a Dream.'"

Now I was very familiar with Dr. King because my family spoke openly about his work, his good as well as others, but no one was like Dr. King, and we shared the same birthday. I was really the cream of the crop then. I would say my birthday is a holiday. They shut down everything on my birthday. This was the beginning of me really loving my birthday. My birthday is still one of the greatest events of my life.

I celebrate many things, but my birthday is a *pure miracle. I am a pure miracle.* I celebrate my gift of life now for the purpose of glorifying God with it and not myself. But I love my birthday. So I worried my mother, my fathers, my brothers with helping me learn this speech.

Oh, my father took me for a new dress and the salon, especially for this speech. I went every other week always, but I really had to go for this speech. I was so eager to speak in front of people.

I wasn't scared at all. I was Dr. King for a day. I nailed my speech. They said to talk loudly. I had no problem with that. I have built-in microphones in me. I am naturally loud like my mother, LOL. After I finished my speech and my teacher told me I did an excellent job, and the audience clapped, I knew at that moment that if I spoke about something important and powerful like Dr. King, people would listen. I set my aim to only talk about or speak about things that mattered most.

I can say that I am still that way today. I don't spend a lot of time talking about foolishness nor people. I understood as a child time is precious here one minute gone that next. I used to hear my family say when someone died, I wish this, and I wish that I could of or would of for the dead person now. And that always bothered me as a child. I would wonder why they didn't do or tell the person how that felt or feel. But it also taught me that people were capable of living a lie and in unbelief, untruth. That they would say one thing in the person's face but something different behind their back. This is what we call being two-faced, unstable, but the Bible called it double-minded. You thinking two different things about one situation, and you have no resolve within yourself. I learned to say what I mean and mean what I say. You will read about it in the coming chapters who taught me this life-changing revelation "to be real" and be who you are all the time.

Caring for Grandma after Dialysis

My grandmother, my mom's mom, was now living with us because she is on dialysis three days a week. Now she has almost twenty grandchildren I think with six to eight around her on a daily basis.

But I am always the one she calls for everything. "Tookie, bring me some water, give me this, take that away. Where is this and where is that?" And my mom would say, "See about Momma 'til I get back." I would be so mad because I wanted to play outside in peace like the other grandchildren.

I would think to myself they're older than me, why they can't help you? I didn't want to get another glass of water or a box of starch or a fruit cup. I didn't want to help her out the cab from dialysis so she could give my brother treats for doing nothing while I do everything for her. But God gave her an eye to see something in me that needed to be nurtured and developed and practiced.

Me, on the other hand, didn't see a purpose, didn't want purpose. I wanted to play like a child. All I remember thinking is why is everybody making me grow up so quick, are they all about to die and leave me alone? What is going on? First, my father with his mother, now my mother with her mother. I did what I was told, with an attitude of course. I received a lot of beatings for my attitude and behavior, my disrespect for my grandmother. She showed favoritism toward us children, and I hated that as did my mother. And, of course, I was the black sheep. They called it the rebel, the hardheaded child, a disrespectful child that talked back and lied to your face. In my mind, I was like, "You don't like me anyway, so why be nice to you? It wasn't gonna change how you felt about me."

I was a horrible child in some areas and nice in others. When I was forced to do something, I was horrible, to say the least. Beatings did nothing for me. I didn't care about that. It was momentarily, but if I refused to obey you, I had the control, and that was what I wanted to be in control of my own life since that was taken from me early.

Made to Cook, Serve, and Entertain Others

My mother loved to cook and entertain guest. I was the only girl, so she just assumed I would love to cook and entertain people. How wrong she was, *I thought*. You know something I spent a lot of years fighting against my mother. If she liked something, I was against it.

If she said red, I said green. I didn't do it verbally all the time. I did it in my behavior, my attitude. I was determined to be 100 percent like my father, so I studied his lifestyle more. And when my mother traits rose up in me, I tried to bury them and did time and time again. But as I got to be an adult, I realized that the very things I hated about my mother, I myself became. All the fighting to avoid being like her, I was becoming her daily. I've seen it, I felt it, I acted like it. My ex-husband told me I was just like my mother. I got mad with him. I began to say to him one time all the things I don't do like my mother and what I do differently from her.

When I finished, he looked at me and said, "Tookie, all that s——you just named off is you."

I was super pissed at him and how could he say that about me? But I began to really pay attention to myself, and like I just said, I became everything I hated. I cried as I always did when I had to face the truth and hurt. I said, "Lord, make me better, make me different, and I strived for better." I would watch how I responded in different situations, and I would say, "Okay, I act like my mom in this way." And then others ways I would say, "I acted like my father in this way," and the rest was myself, my own personality and traits.

This was why I could tell you who I got what from with my parents and what was a learned behavior or my way of being. When I tell you I study myself, I really do because I was messed up completely, and I had to know did I cause all the drama of the life I was living or was it dealt with me. And I found the truth, but you will read about that in volume 4 *The Heart of the Matter: God Cleansing My Insides and Me Facing Truth about Myself.*

Now back to the story at hand, excuse me y'all, I just like talking to you. Once again, God showed my mom purpose in me in an area that He would use later. Oh, no one could decorate like my mother.

Oh my goodness, she goes all out for the holidays and events. Christmas, we got a real tree, she has red and green curtains, couch covers, rugs, and she loves wallpaper. Good lord, this woman loves wallpaper. Thanksgiving, she changes the house brown and orange. Halloween, we have pumpkins and costumes, candy the whole nine yards. She made curtains and bedspreads. I used to love sewing with my grandmother now. That was one thing I loved—to cut old clothes and sew to make blankets with her. She was nice then. But my mother would cook for days to prepare for her events. I would have to make the trays, peel potatoes, frost the cakes, and I hated it all.

Because I was made to do it all the time, I despised cooking and decorating, just leave me be. I would think to myself. I said out loud a lot and got beaten for my mouth. Once again, I didn't care.

But God is using all of it now. I absolutely love to cook, entertain, and decorate. And what is surprising, I loved it before I left home, LOL. We, as people, are fickle at best, I am telling you, but my God surrounded me in a family that would nurture and cultivate all the gifts and talents he placed in me and was strong enough to make me obey them and wasn't afraid to *beat the brakes off me.*

CHAPTER 3

WHAT CAN I DO TO HELP?

I am still the one my grandma calls to help her out the cab and bring water or whatever. She really is much sicker now, so I don't give her a really hard time about helping out. I still help with my other grandmother as well. My father brings her to Illinois now, that was great to me. I help her on the weekends when I go visit my father. I am still going to school like a good little girl. I am still attending Awana faithfully and church most Sundays. I miss church when I am with my real father because I go with him sometimes. Other times, we might be on the highway late at night; it all depends on my father's mood for the weekend. Either way, I am just happy to be with him.

Grandma Is Gone

My grandmother becomes sicker something with her heart. They did some type of surgery I'm not really sure, but it is dealing with her heart. My mom and all her siblings are very worried about Grandma and this surgery. I am not really sure how long after, but Grandma passed in the hospital. My mom had just left there or got home or something, but they came, told her that Grandma was dead. I still remember my mother crying, oh god. I came in the living room like, "What? Oh my god."

We all began to cry. I began to pray, "Lord, please bring Grandma back. I will be a good girl. I will not complain about all the times she calls me. I will help her out the cab. Please, please don't take her from us. My mom needs her. My family needs her."

Well, Grandma was gone. In the coming days, I heard my mom and family talk about how they think the doctor messed up during Grandma's surgery. And the funeral home told them that they found a needle that the hospital left in Grandma's heart from the surgery. From that day, I hated that hospital and would not trust doctors. They killed my grandma. I told all my cousins that they killed Grandma. They say, "How do you know?"

I said, "Because I heard my mother tell the family they left a needle in Grandma's heart from the surgery. We cannot go back to that hospital y'all or believe doctors, okay?"

My cousins, they listened, but I don't think they believed what I was saying. But my mind was made up. I dare not to go to that hospital. I lived by this rule until I was nineteen years old. I was shopping at the mall with my mom when I had a pain in my stomach so strong I fell to my knees. My mother called my father. He came and got us.

He said, "I am taking you to the closest hospital."

I was lying on the back seat. I said, "No, take me to Riverside," because the hospital that killed my grandma was the first one, but I dare not tell my father that. My father never liked hospitals only the VA when he would go to rest.

I never understood that about him. He never would come into the hospital to see us or the babies, but he comes to the hospital all the times and stay outside and send others in to bring him a report.

To let us know he is outside, I witnessed my father do this all my life. He would be the first to arrive in an emergency situation for all of us or his friends, family. He truly loved hard and was gonna be there for you, but not in the hospital whether at the hospital parking lot. He would spend the day talking to all the people coming and going, LOL. It is so funny now that I write about it and think about my father. He never meets a stranger, never ever.

But he told me, "Baby, I am taking you to the closest one so they can see what is wrong with you."

He drove me straight to the killers. I looked up at the hospital. I said, "Noooo, they'll gonna kill me like they did to Grandma."

My mother said, "What you say?"

I said, "They'll gonna kill me like they did to Grandma. They left a needle in her heart and killed her."

My mother said, "You remember that?"

I said, "Yes"—crying—"please don't make me go in."

Well, my father told them to put me on the stretcher and go see about his baby, see what is wrong with his baby.

I already knew he would be outside the entire time. They wheeled me in and told me that my gallstones had started to release into my body, and I needed surgery, exactly two surgeries because I was stuck in my bile duct, and they needed to remove that one first then remove my gallbladder.

But the real issue came in when they could not do either one until my system was free of cocaine. I said to the doctor, "Please don't tell my parents. It would kill them after they kill me." I told him, "I had just started going to a party over the weekend you know like teenagers."

He said, "I am only doing this because you have three children. Your children need you. Stop this right now."

I said, "Yes, sir, thank you. I will."

So when my mom came in, the doctor said, "We're keeping Antonette. She has had a gallstone attack, and the stones are releasing and stuck in the bile duct. Once we stabilize her pain level, then I will do first surgery in three days, and then the next surgery the next day. She will be here about five days if she cooperates," and he looked at me.

I said, "You have my word. I will listen. Just stop me from hurting."

They took me to my room that night. My mom was staying at my father's house while I was in the hospital. Oh god, I was scared to death. All I could think about was this the room my grandma died in? I would not go to sleep for the first night. The second night they gave me so much medication I went to sleep, no food or anything so I could have the surgery. I got up the next morning, 6:00 a.m., for surgery, brushing my teeth, and I was in the bathroom looking in the mirror, and I left my body. I was walking on what looked like clouds with my aunt, Aunt Honey we called her, my grandma's sister that passed recently. I was close to her too.

She said, "Tookie, don't be scared. You will be fine, just fine."

I returned to my body. I was still looking in the mirror with my toothbrush in my hand. There was peace in my hospital room. I had no fear at all. I knew my grandma was okay, and I could trust these doctors. They performed both surgeries successfully, and I was released to go home. I went home, and my cousin stayed to continue to care for my three children because I wasn't well at all. I could barely walk from all the pain in my stomach.

At this time in my life, I was a huge fan of horoscopes and psychics. I wanted to know what was going to happen, and I did like surprises or changes to my plans. I liked to stick to my routine and plans. So I called the psychic, and he said, "Antonette, I have a message for you from your grandmother."

My hairs stood up on my head. He said, "She said she was with you at the hospital. She never left you. And she is very proud of you. Don't have any guilt concerning her. She loves you and has always loved you. Go ahead and live a good life. You have many great years ahead. You live life with no regrets. Goodbye."

He told me a few other things that violated my life, and from that day to this one, I began to live my life with *no regrets*. I never called another psychic after that day. That freed me on so many levels I could begin to explain. But if I make a decision, and it works in my favor or not, I didn't waddle in regret because I make my own decisions. Therefore, I don't blame anyone for anything that goes right or wrong in my life. I am free from people's opinions and expectations of me.

What Can I Do to Help?

After Grandma died, I noticed that I was surrounded by many sick people. I guess I began to look for the sick people to help to remember to help Grandma. But I noticed many sick and ill people in my family, in our community. I noticed all our family and friends getting sick from drinking and using drugs, which was a huge sickness and disease. So I would help watch children. Gave my clothes away when I got new ones, which was weekly. My mother used to give them away, and I cried, but now I give her clothes to help people. I gave her all my toys, except for my dolls. I couldn't give away my babies. When I was at school, if I saw a child being picked on or bullied, I fought for them. I hated to see people mistreated. If I heard people talking about someone, I would jump in and stop them. When my Grandma died, it awakened a desire and passion in me that I never had. I like it, say it birthed a passion in me. Passion for the sick, the disabled, the diseased, the addicts, the drunkards, the less fortunate—they all needed help in some way. That is when I realized that all people are alike. It had nothing to do with color, age, status, money, gender, smarts, knowledge, job or no job, happy or sad. Boy or girl or where you lived, we all had a need for help. When I saw this, it created another question in my mind. Well, if we all have a need of some kind no matter where we are or who we are, then how can I help?

How can I help the people on drugs? How can I help the people that drinks? How can I help the children that don't have a father? How can I help the elderly lady? How can I help the sick man? How can I help the children that are sad? I asked all these questions daily. Seemed like for months and years. I prayed, I asked my parents, my camp leaders, my teachers. I would not, could not, let it go. This really worried me. I would lay in bed and talk to Jesus every day asking him what about this person and what about that person? Did you see how sad they were? Were you with them like you with me? Do you hear them and talk to them like you do with me? And every day I would go see if the people I prayed for was better because I knew prayer worked. And if the people were still sick, I asked what they needed me to do for them. I helped them and continued to talk to Jesus daily about helping the people, helping them children.

This was when I began to give away almost everything I had and would make my father buy the children the stuff he bought for me. I would say they need it. They would ask for my favorite toys or clothes, and I would say, "I will get my daddy to get you one." And I would. And I continued this way of life until I got about thirty when the Lord told me to start buying what people asked me for instead of giving them mine.

Now when He said this, I thought I was hearing things, but I wasn't. So what I would do was when I purchased something for me that I thought someone would ask for, I purchased two at a time. So I would be obeying God still. He allowed me to operate in that foolishness for about three or four months. When He said, "I told you to give them your own personal items that you loved and got for yourself." I was instantly upset at first, but the Lord taught me a valuable lesson about obeying him the first time, exactly the way He tells me. The Lord had told me to give my gospel collection of CDs to this man in my church Old St. John in Wesson, Mississippi, named Howard. Howard loved gospel music, but Howard became very sick and didn't have a lot of money. The pastor would pick him and his wife up for church and Bible study. So one Bible study, Howard talked about gospel music, and he was saying, "Oh boy, I wished I could meet this person and that person. I love this song and that song. I wait for it to play on the radio."

And the Lord said to me, "Give Howard your twenty CDs collection."

I was like, "I just bought that collection because I gave my mother the extra set."

So Sunday came, I didn't give it to Howard. I could not rest or listen to the collection, hoping Jesus would change his mind. So when Wednesday came, I gave Howard my twenty CDs collection against my own will but according to God's perfect will."

He lit up like a Christmas tree. He hugged me so tight. He was in tears. He said, "Oh, God bless you. Oh boy, I'm going to listen to all of these."

Howard was so happy. I wasn't happy because I didn't want to give away my own collection. I wanted to purchase him a collection like I did with my mother, what was the difference? And I let Howard know this was my very own private collection he was getting. Well, two Wednesdays later, Howard went to be with the Lord, and his wife said he was at peace listening to those CDs I had given to him.

That moment changed the course of my giving and obedience to God. I still think about that Howard each time the Lord told me to give something away or sow a seed of money or my time with someone I act as if it's is my last opportunity to do good unto them and unto God. I still ask the Lord every day, "*What can I do to help?*"

CHAPTER 4

GIVEN A SOLUTION

I go to church one Sunday, and they announced that Mrs. Trudie was going back to Trinidad, and JoJo was going to the Philippines to continue to be missionaries to bring help and hope to the helpless. And it hit me. I want to help the helpless and hopeless. And I began to pray that very moment that God would give me a job that I could always help the sick people, and the desire to become a nurse was birthed in me. I thought to myself, *Yes, this is it.*

I will be a nurse and travel missionary to help sick people all over the world. I already had a love for travel and the highway from my father. I said, "Yes, this is the perfect plan." As I began to look around the church, I noticed that Reverend Williams and Mrs. Williams worked in ministry together.

Then their children all worked in the ministry with their wives and children. Their son Mark, he and his wife, Karen, worked for the ministry. Mark drove the church van and worked with the boys.

Karen played the piano and worked with the children ministry. Mark's twin Mary worked full time in the ministry over several departments and lived full time on campus. She was over the Awana Clubs when we traveled, and she also did missionary work with travel. They were training their children to work in ministry and give their lives to Christ at an early age. So that idea was birthed in me as well.

I said, "Lord, this is the solution to my problem. How I can help all these people that are sick and hurting?"

I go to sleep and either I dream or received a revelation of my future. I am not completely sure how I received this revelation of my future, but I did. The future promise of my destiny was that I would marry a pastor of a church, to become a pastor's wife. I would have a daughter, and I would travel a lot to ministry to help the sick and hurting all over the world.

I saw myself in Africa, China, and the Philippines and throughout the United States of America.

I would do extensive travel with my husband after my child was grown because I just saw my husband and I was traveling a lot to do the work of the Lord. We both loved the Lord Jesus and being a blessing to His people. We lived by faith. I never worried about our needs. We were established and rooted in faith in God. I am not sure if he, my husband, grew up in Bible witness camp, but we both had a strong foundation of faith from our childhoods. As I grew older, this desire and passion in me increased. I continued to learn of Christ daily. I continued to help all I came in contact with through my parents, school, church, and Awana. I now understand this scripture. I now understand that the daughter of Zion must be made. And this would not begin my process to be made, but rather I would continue in being made.

> And I will make her that Halted a remnant, and her that was cast far off a strong nation: and the Lord shall reign over them in Zion from henceforth, even for ever. (Micah 4:7, KJV)

I was given this scripture during the writing of my first book series. When the Lord was making and molding me into the woman I am today, he began to give me scriptures that I might understand my past, present, and future to see that He was always with me from a child. He gave this scripture to help me understand that He designed me to be strong—"a strong nation," meaning I will be able to handle people of all sorts. I had to go through my process of feeling not loved to be able to give love, my process of rejection, that I might receive all that come to me, my process of being misunderstood, that I might have understanding and insight, my season of lack that I might become a giver, my season of silent that I might become a listener, my season of talking that I might speak words of eternal life. All the ups and downs, the mishaps, misfortunes, abuse, misuse, setbacks, delays, broken promises, dead dreams, lack of vision, unknown purpose or destiny, all was a part of my process to becoming a daughter of Zion, a remnant "leftovers," cast away that God was building and preparing for His end-time army. All things, all things, all things work together for them that are thee called according to His purpose and plan. Glory be to God in the Highest.

Don't despise your process to greatness no matter how it looks or feels. Stay at the feet of Jesus. Cast your cares on Him because He cared for you. And surely, don't be like the people of Israel—"complainers." You will never receive your promise or enter the promised land if you are a complainer and despise the process, the plan, the path, the journey, the road, the cross God has chosen for you to get you to your destiny with is your destination. So my dear hearts, be of good cheer. God loves you so much. He sent Jesus to redeem us and the Holy Spirit to guide us. You have all the help and tools you need to succeed. Use them wisely. Complete your course in this life that you may reign here now and there later. Prepare yourself for the kingdom.

CHAPTER 5

WHO I AM ASSIGNED TO?

Trained by My Father to Evangelize

Now it was never documented nor put in books or on paper, but my belief with all my heart and my sisters agree that our father was a true evangelist. My father never, never meet a stranger.

He talked and helped all he came in contact with. He would get up each day to go look for people to help and bless. Like I said before, I was late in life baby. My father was in his fifties when he made me, and I was born. So I didn't know him in his younger years, but my sisters and brothers said my father didn't play. He was very serious and struck with them growing up. They received beatings, not spankings, from our father. But I don't know that side of him and so glad I don't. I always say that my father loved me a little too much because he protected me in so many ways and made me feel as if the world was at my feet to serve me. That I would be and have anything I wanted in this life.

Nothing or no one was off limits to me. I had access to all things. Well, that is partial truth because when I began to live for the kingdom of God, that was the first thing God had to break me from—this philosophy that was embedded into me that I witnessed with my own eyes work. That I myself had personally experienced this notion to be true in many forms. It took Jesus years to deliver me from this very truth I believed. I say it is partial truth because we, at one point, were given the world because God us dominion over the earth, but because of the fall of Adam, we lose it. But Jesus got it back. Now we, as humans, are recovering our crowns and dominion daily if we walk as Jesus walked, but that's whole other topic of discussion.

My father began to really take me with him more and more on his outreach missions—I now call them since I have a better understanding of my life. He would talk to me as we drove all over to help people. He would say be nice, be respectful, be a lady, and you are a lady, act like one. Stop being so rough and tomboyish. I was a tomboy. I climbed trees, played football, tackle, ran, jumped off buildings. It drove my father crazy, LOL, because he would take me to get my hair done each week, take me shopping for new clothes, buy me dresses because I loved dresses. He would get me all fixed up and pretty, and I go outside and turn flips in my dress, play in the mud and rain. He would just look at me and shake his head.

"You're not going with me looking like that," he would say.

I would fake cry, and he waited for me to change clothes. I was his baby, what can I say? But we delivered groceries to countless people house. We took clothes to children, even took some shopping with us. Now I was fond of that part because now you invading my place and time with my father. I didn't like for others to come with us, especially children. My father would pick up his grandchildren who called him daddy. All my father grandchildren called him daddy because he was very active and present in all their lives. I felt some kind of way about that because I felt they stole time away from me his child, but I dare not say that. But once again, this is behind the scenes, the attitudes and secret thoughts I dealt with quietly. But my father was so happy to serve everyone. He paid light bills, water bills, rent, and you name it for countless people. He helped the fatherless, the widowed, the homeless, the drug addicts, the loss, the confused, the teen parents, the orphans, the runaways, the strays, the gays, the disabled, the list goes on and on, and all that fell in between.

I don't recall not coming in contact with people of all ages, races, stages, careers, jobs, status, or cultures that we didn't help. My father traveled a lot, so we were in contact with many cultures, people of different status. Doctors, lawyers, nurses, business owners, we were an integrated family. I have Polish nieces and nephews, white, German, Indian, and African American. Our community was integrated of all cultures, and we all had needs of some sorts. My parents housed Caucasian children in our home for years. There were no he-white or she-black mess in our home.

In our community, the church we all grew up in was ran by Caucasian family—the Williams who I love dearly. My uncles married Caucasian women and had children; my brothers did as well. We were not taught to be prejudice as far as cultures and race. My parents have had relationships with other cultures as well as myself. Some of our family members don't go that far as we did because they believe in mating with your own kind, and I did too until the Lord confronted my prejudice in mating with other races. Dating yes, mating was no, but now I will do both. See, we can be prejudice to certain areas of our lives unconsciously and don't realize it until you meet pure truth and His name is JESUS. He brings all things to the light because he is light. But for many years, I watched my father helped thousands of people of all cultures, and he did this all his entire life. He gave of himself and resources until it hurt him. And it really did in the end. As you know and have read in *The Real Antonette Come Forth Series* that my father could not read or write, but God naturally gifted Him. He owned several businesses and started them from nothing—I mean nothing.

He was a self-made man, one would call him. He would strategize a business plan and at the speed of thought and carry it out, will have others to carry out the paperwork, but the plan was his. The organization, building, location, office, business transactions, meetings, network all was done by my father. He had wisdom from above, and the tongue of the learned for sure. He knew people and how to deal with people no doubt he had signs and wonders that followed him daily. Everyone loved him—to know him is to love him. Jentle was his name, and he was just that gentle. But due to his lack of education and lack thereof, he sold drugs to fund his and start his businesses, I am assuming. I don't know how he came to know that life, but it was before my time, and he brought me into it out of fear. He wanted to assure I could take care of myself before he died. He had a near-death experience, so he wanted to prepare me. My father didn't have faith in me getting a husband to take care of me.

He said, "I want to make sure you can take care of yourself because I don't know what kind of husband you will get. But I don't want you to have to depend on anyone for anything." And he taught me his ways good and bad. They could never catch my father with drugs of any kind. He would always be a step ahead of them. I think this was because he had a heart of gold and was good for people. He gave God what was due to Him regardless of how he obtained the money. My father paid tithes and gave offerings to churches. I also learned that from him too. God knows all and sees all. So they knew my father had a love for cars. He loved brand-new cars and trucks off the showroom floors. But he also would obtain cars for payments of drugs he gave people on credit when they couldn't pay their debts to him.

So one year in 1997, they gave my father two cars for drug payments—both were stolen. He was arrested driving one.

They put him in jail with a high bond for months. Because they could not pin drugs on him, they set him up with cars. Well, he got out of jail finally, but a year and a half or two, they sentenced him to time in prison. They set him up for another case, not even sure what it was exactly, but he got eight to ten years I think. I was devastated, so that's why I can't really remember the times and dates. But my father died in prison five years later of a heart attack. I never saw him alive again. Once he went to prison, I was twenty-two years old. I had just birthed my fourth child when they sentenced, my mother and my children's father all in a few months. My father ended his life in prison because his love and desire to help people was stronger than his love and desire for Christ was at that time.

But in my heart of hearts, I feel like my father turned his whole heart to Christ in prison because he was in his older years. He had shared the prison with two of his sons. My sisters were visiting him on the regular, ministering the gospel of Jesus Christ to him because my two oldest sisters had become an evangelist and accredited all to our father. He lived to see the fruits of his labor with his children, grandchildren, great-grandchildren, and even great-great-grandchildren. He was a blessed man beyond his strength. God showed him the honor of honoring him. I knew for a fact my father prayers saved my life. Months after his death, I was gone. I mean gone in my mind on drugs. I had lost the one man that loved me. My father was my everything. I was high-strung on cocaine, heroin, marijuana, pills, alcohol some of it all. Then I was arrested in for multiple warrants for stealing and missing court. As I sat in Chicago Cook County Department of Correction on the suicide floor with no bond. The Lord sent this minister to minister to us. They narrowed me to attend this church service since I had finally stopped crying after days of incarceration.

During this man's sermon, he said to us, I said it was for me, but he looked at me, and he said, "God has honored your father's prayers on his deathbed. You were here because your father asked God to please save his daughter. 'Please save my daughter,' so, woman, I want you to know that God has answered someone's dying wish to save their daughters, their granddaughters. Take this opportunity and honor those that honored you as they left this earth. They had you on their minds. All they were concerned about was you as they died, not themselves. That is the gospel that saves."

As that man spoke, tears rolled down my face because I know that was my father's and my grandmother's dying wish and prayers that God would save me. At that moment, I felt their love and strength within me. I, to the Lord, I promise I will live for you for honoring my father's death prayers and saving me.

I thanked the minister, and that was the last service they allowed us to attend because of lockdown.

They released me from Cook County Jail on December 24, 2002. I went to my mom, spent Christmas with my children, turned myself into Kankakee County Jail as I promised Jesus I would serve seven more days there then released, returned to my job, got an apartment, and relapsed on drugs.

On March 3, 2003, I left Kankakee, Illinois, a fugitive on the run for twelve years, but I served my Lord Jesus fully from that day to this. I lived for Him and honored my father, grandmother's dying prayers of saving me. This has been a steady sixteen-year journey of greatness. I have experienced many hardships, up and downs, but I am staying the course. Yes, times got hard, and my way was rocky. I drew from and still drew from the strengths of my ancestors. I go to their graves for wisdom, for strength to stand and to pray for their guidance. No doubt in my mind that they are with me every step of the way. This is how I began to understand who I am assigned too, to help. You must understand that we are called to do many things, chosen for others, and designed for the rest.

Seek Christ. He will reveal your call, your assignment, and your destiny to you by way of revelation, dreams, visions, prophecy, or word of knowledge, and time travel. God will take you back to your past to show you things He has imparted into you. Wow, I just realized that this is how He has done me with my life testimony. He took me back to my past and brought me full circle to now that I might actively and effectively write my life testimony. Thank you, Apostle David E. Taylor, my spiritual father of Joshua Media Ministries International (JMMI) of Taylor, Michigan. He has been teaching us about time travel, being a glory gift and manifestation God is doing to teach us His ways.

He takes you to the past, the future, trips to heaven, and trips to hell for us to learn the kingdom and learn about our kingship powers and dominion. Oh my god, I really just realize that God has been allowing the Holy Spirit to time travel me in my past. It was like I knew He brought a lot of things to my remembrance because, of course, I buried a lot of things to survive. So I never dealt with any of it until God began my deliverance process. This is amazing. This is powerful. Wow. I am in awe. Our God is great. He is wonderful. This is the Holy Spirit living through you to fulfill God's will for your life, and you do not know it. Apostle has taught on this subject too that how I am able to realize it.

This is a powerful revelation. It is 3:00 a.m., and I am in my hotel room writing this book. I can only write when instructed by

God, and He is not bound by time or circumstances. I will be hosting the Empowerment Ministry Mississippi Youth Group Administration and Etiquette Class in just a few hours. I am truly in the glory realm right now. It's wonderful.

OMG—operating in mega glory as Bishop George Scott says. This is powerful, people. I got to stop writing and praise God. I am taking a victory praise break. Glory be to God.

CHAPTER 6

PROVISION GIVEN

I am still attending Awana Camp on Wednesdays, church on Sundays, maybe twice a month because I am still going with my father's on the weekend. I still go to Mississippi on Christmas breaks. I haven't stayed in the summer in a few years. We go for about one week or so. A lot is going on with me in my personal life. Molestation is at an all-time high; grown men are now becoming more regular. I have to do something before my virginity is taken. It is getting harder to fight them off.

This is when I decide to look for a boyfriend to get me a baby, so I can move out to my mom's house.

In the meantime, I am being trained by my father to be my own boss and work for myself. He is the master of entrepreneurship. Now he had already been teaching me the business of drugs.

How to measure, cook, and bag cocaine. First, it was powder cocaine then it became rock cocaine.

I went with him to purchase large quantities and learn how to weigh it on the scale, then how to hide it to get home. I hid it on my body because I was a child and a girl. The police wasn't allowed to search children or females back in those days. Times has really changed because now they search babies and all. Thank God He delivered me from the lifestyle many years ago. So no matter if I finished school or go to college, I had provision that would take care of myself and children if I decided to have them without the help of a man in my life. My father thought he was dying soon, so he wanted to make sure I could maintain the lifestyle I was accustom to, afforded by him without the hassle of a man or relationship.

Day Care Provision

My mother and her sisters liked to go out more now. So all of them have children, some of us were older and some were younger. My mom's baby sister was still having children like roaches. But she wanted to hang with my mom, and so do my mom's friends. So they paid me to babysit. My mom told them I was responsible enough to care for a newborn baby, and I was. So my aunt left her children with me—her oldest was my age—but would not watch the baby. I watched him. He was three months at the time. You talked about a beautiful child. This child was beautiful. I watched him for about two months every other weekend until tragedy hit our lives.

The first tragedy was the death of my seventeen-year-old brother. He was killed in a car accident and killed instantly. Our lives were changed forever. My family really started to come over a lot to see about my mom. She wasn't taking his death well at all. So one of my aunts moved in with us. I helped watch her children too when her oldest would not watch them. I watched my mom's best friend three children in her home on weekdays, weekends, because she and my mom was very close. A few months after my brother's death, my aunt's baby that I used to babysit was hit in the head with a wooden broom during a fight by his parents. I think he was about four or five months old at the time. The blow was so hard it cracked his skull, and he was hospitalized for months.

The Department of Children and Family Services took my aunt's other children, the five other, at the time of this accident. She fought for months to get them back, and she did, but never got her baby back. He was adopted by another family, but she remained in contact with him throughout his life until her death. He grew and knew all his siblings as of today. But that affected me deeply because I loved that baby, and I wasn't allowed to see him in the hospital because I was a child myself. So I continued to babysit my mom's best friend three children when she asked, which was regular. This is where I first noticed my future husband watching me as I played outside with the children in the front yard, and he would be passing on his horse—he trained horses. I would see him pass when I was home. They bought the property next door to our home. So I would see him pass all the time. One year later, he asked me for my number, and the rest is history. You can read about us in *The Real Antonette Come Forth Series*. That is too much to talk about now. But one weekend, I went to stay with my father, and my mom and her best friend wanted to go out, so her friend left her children home alone. I think the oldest girl was about seven, the other girl four, and the boy three.

Well, tragedy struck our lives again. When the mother left, as she always did, the oldest would have to watch and care for the younger two children. And like children do, they cry when their parents leave them. They would cry when she left them with me. That's why she always wanted them to be in their own home and environment. She loved her children, but that weekend was horrible. I was out of town with my father. The oldest sister was babysitting the younger siblings, and the little girl began to cry for her mother. She cried for hours sometimes. The sister wanted her to shut up and stop crying and she would not. She looked for my mom to come home soon. She didn't. Well, the oldest daughter took a pillow and placed it over the younger sister's head to make her stop crying and screaming, and she suffocated her sister. The four-year-old died. The mom returned home hours later to find her daughter dead and the other children still in the home watching TV. When she noticed her daughter not breathing, she called 911.

She asked her oldest daughter what happen to her baby. At first, the oldest said she thought she was sleep. But when the coroner performed the autopsy, he concluded that the child had been suffocated and dead for over four hours. The police were called, and the other children removed from the home. When the police questioned the mother, she said she had gone to the store down the street, and her sister was supposed to watch her children that lived next door. But that wasn't true. She never helped with those children. The Department of Children and Family Services removed the children from her care. When the police questioned the oldest daughter and the little boy, they found out the mother left them home alone all the time. The oldest daughter told the police she told her mother don't leave them home alone.

She told them that her sister always cried, and she wanted her to shut, up and she would not. She told the police that she put the pillow over her head until she stopped crying and breathing. She hated her family. Poor child. They put her in a juvenile home until she was eighteen years old for the murder of her sister because she knew she was killing her with the pillow. This child was under tremendous stress at the time. But the mother never regained custody of her nor the son. Family members stepped in and raised the son while the daughter was in prison. The mother became a full-blown drug addict. She used to drink, but after this tragedy, she really lost what mind she had. She and my mother still remained friends even more because they were like sisters, trying to help each other. They allowed the mother to talk to her oldest daughter to see what really happened, and the daughter told her mom she's glad she killed her sister, and she was next. This robbed the mother to the core because the girl's father family fueled her with hate for her mother. But the girl served her time in jail I think nine to ten years. Beautiful children. The mother got better over time to the best of her ability. She remained close to the son. They are all grown now with children both of them, and their mom is a great grandmother to her grandchildren. They're happy regardless of the past. So this is how my training for childcare. Day care provision was birthed and practiced.

Real Estate Provision

So my father is always buying this house, that house, this building, that building, and renovating them to be whatever he need them for. The renovation of stores, gas stations, houses was nonending with him. And I am right at his side with my input of questions. I think I got on my father's nerve because I asked so many questions, but he didn't ever tell me to stop. But my mom, would in minute, she would say, "Don't question me. Just do what I say."

I would say, "Well, how am I supposed to question? You say don't question you and don't question God?" I said, "I'll just ask my daddy. He knows."

She would get mad and say, "Your daddy don't know anything. You think he knows everything."

I would say, "He does, and he will tell me." That was the truth, and he would. So as a child, I always loved wood. I was always building, cutting, and decorating something with wood. Paint, wire, I just loved to create things for my room. I made wood shelves for my dolls. I built a baby bed for my dolls and took to school for show-and-tell. I was so mad the teacher gave me a B for my dollhouse. She doesn't know how many days it took me to get that doll bed built. How many pieces of wood I cut wrong, how many times I hit my fingers with the hammer, trying to nail the fence around the bed for railing. My mother would try to get me to do it differently, but I wanted to create what I saw, and I did. This is how I began my desire and training for real estate provision.

Hairdresser

As I use to babysit all the children, I loved to comb the babies hair. I loved to bath them and wash their hair, be it in ponytails and braids. The little girls I would put beads on their hair. My aunt, my uncle's wife, used to braid my cousin's hair and put beads on their heads. Now my mom's sister used the same beads for door dividers or room dividers. Back in those days, my aunt had all kinds of strings of colored beads hanging in her doorways through her house. But my uncle's wife used them to decorate her daughter's head. She put the beads on fishing stings to get on braids of hair.

This is where I learned to put beads on hair. I practice with my many dolls. My father purchased me all kinds of beads. My mom showed me how to braid. When I was an at-home mom for my first three children, I did braids at home of many kinds. This is how I started to train for my provision as a hairdresser.

Event Planner and Cook

As a child, I was my mother only girl and her baby. She loved to entertain and decorate as I told you earlier in this book. She used to make me do the trays for her events, set the table with decor.

I hated all of it because I didn't like all these people coming over, and I had to clean up after they left and went home. Oh yes, they would all come to eat and party and go home. And I was left cleaning up after them while my brothers that were older than me watching TV, play video games, or play outside. I was so angry about this all the time because my mother never made them clean our house or wash clothes—I did it all. All they had to do was take the trash out after I cleaned up and bring wood inside for our fireplace. I had to wash and hand their clothes. So I started throwing their clothes and shoes away if they left them in the living and dining room. They got mad and told my mother I threw their shoes and pants in the garbage. She yelled and screamed, whooped me several times. I didn't care. I told to keep it off the floor. I am not a maid.

They and my mother knew I didn't care about getting a whooping. They didn't break me. I was determined to have control no matter the cost I had to pay. And it paid off because my brothers began to keep their clothes and shoes in their rooms, and I definitely wasn't apologizing for throwing them away. But because my mother made me cook and decorate the home and tables, prepare fruit, cheese, meats, and vegetable trays, make dessert dishes, I now am very good at it all. I have almost every color dinner napkins, table runner, and napkin rings. I can plan an event dinner party, award dinner pastors, anniversary dinner, etiquette classes, and decorate my home like it is a museum. This is how I began my provision as an event planner because I was made to do it as a child.

Cooking

My aunt (Viola), my second mom that had me from four weeks old. She taught me to cook from the heart. She would tell me to take my time and prepare my children a meal. She would say, "You are what you eat." If you feed a child junk food, that is what they will act like. If you feed a child fast food, that is what they will act like. If you take your time and prepare a hot home-cooked meal for your child, they would behave like somebody and be good. And the same for a man, if you feed him, he will act right.

I listened and said, "I hate cooking because my mom made me cook."

She said, "Well, you need to learn to cook for your children because I am not cooking for you every day." And she began my cooking classes from the heart. She said, "You have to love to cook for people to enjoy your food. Your attitude is in your food. You can be in a bad mood and cook and think your family will enjoy your meal."

At first, I was like, "Now, Aunt, all this isn't necessary to fry chicken. Give me a break."

So she said, "You decide what you want to learn to cook, and I will show you."

So I loved my aunt crowder peas, field peas, and corn bread. So she told me to always get fresh vegetables, fresh eggs, and fruit. She told me what brand seasonings to use, milk, butter, oil, and pots and pans. Cooking was an art. She was a caterer. She had a cake shop at one time. So I am still that way today about my pots, pans, and seasoning and foods. I was taught by the *best*. We peeled the fresh crowder peas, washed them, and bagged them in freezer bags for later use. She showed me how to shuck corn and cut off the cob to store in the freezer. Collard greens, cabbage, we cleaned, stored, and cooked them all.

My biggest accomplishment was when I learned to make brown gravy. OMG, it took me over a year to make gravy correctly. My aunt would say, "No, ma'am, that isn't right," or "That isn't good." She didn't lie about my cooking. If it wasn't right or missing something, she would say, "That's not right. Try again." I messed up a lot of food, but I think I have mastered a few dishes along the way. I learned to make homemade cakes, pies, and pudding. I have cooked and fed thousands of people in my community because I love to cook. The kitchen was one of my happy places. My children laughed at me because when I came to their homes, the kitchen was the first place I went and began to wash dishes and talk to them. I started cleaning in the kitchen. I have purchased all three of my daughters' cookware, dishes, and cutlery sets for their homes, so when I came to visit and cook at their homes, I would have good pots and pans to prepare them meals.

I cooked at all my children homes and at my mom's too. They put in their request for their meals. I went to purchase all my own foods and ingredients to assure my food was superb for my babies. My grandchildren now called me to place their food orders, and to go cook for her babies. This truly was my happy place, and nothing brought me more joy than to watch them eat and enjoy the foods I cooked from my heart. All my friends and church members loved my cooking and enjoyed my heartfelt meals because they too knew that I cooked from the heart or not at all. I have hosted many friend luncheons, friend dinners, women dinner parties and luncheons, cookouts, parties, and BBQs all because my aunt taught me the art of cooking from my heart. This is how I began my passion as a cook.

CHAPTER 7

CHARACTER DEVELOPMENT AND ATTRIBUTES PROCESS

"Life Process"

I n this chapter, I will walk you through my life journey as I learned and developed my character. I learned from the best and the greatest people on the planet earth to me. I always have said and shown gratitude toward all those that have been a blessing to me. I began to realize that I was very special to my Father Jehovah because He allowed me to sit at the feet of great wisdom. The people He placed in my life and me around I learned from them all. The good, the bad, and the ugly. Now I already told you about the bad and the ugly in *After the Pain* book no. 2 of this series, and I will share more in book 4, *The Heart of the Matter: God Cleansing My Insides and Me Facing Truth about Myself.* This book, my life as a caregiver, is the strength of my joy. This is my happy book, my joyous book even though I really had to go through a mental and emotional cleansing and releasing process before I was able to write this book. You ask why? Well, the majority of the people I honor throughout this book are deceased now, and it still felt like yesterday that they left me. I didn't know if you know this or not, but I would assume you didn't.

Golden nugget for you—when you are a caregiver of any kind, whether by trade, chance, choice, or force, you are investing yourself into that person or people. Each time you perform an act or duty in caring for someone, you develop a bond, a relationship, an emotional attachment, a mental attachment to that person or people. It doesn't matter how you became the one caring for them or whether you like it or dislike your role as a caregiver. One or more of these attachments will take place. Each time you come in contact with that person, you are making and receiving a deposit at the same time. You giving of your time, energy, and emotion to them, and they're receiving or rejecting it. They're giving you their attention, advice, complaint, or praise during your time together. So it is a give-and-take change between two people or a group of people.

Once you have invested yourself into a human being and that human being invests themselves into you, a bond is formed; love is formed. Once you or the person exit each other's life, whether by job change or death, you now have a void in your life, in your heart, in your mind, in your emotion. You go through withdrawals from not being with the person or people. It is just like you ending a marriage or love affair. When you break up or end a romantic relationship with someone, you miss them. Whether the relationship was good or bad, you miss something about them—usually the part of them that brought you joy and laughter, the happy places. But when they leave or you leave their life, you take apart of them with you. Or they take a part of you with them. Your emotional and mental response is the same whether you quit the job, got fired, or they died on you. You will grieve. There are five stages of grief, and there is no time frame for either of them. Sometimes it takes weeks, months, years or decade for you to recover from the grief of the loss of the relationship. You don't know the difference in hurt from a breakup, hurt from rejection, or hurt from a death. All it knows is the pain, loss, and a void, so it grieves because it is missing something. The very thing that brings it joys. This is why people grieve themselves to death every day because they don't understand the stages of grief are the same for all loss of human life through different circumstances. So allow me to share the stages of grief with you that you might understand why I had to process before writing this book.

Grief Five Stages Are DABRA

Denial—refusal to admit the truth or reality of something. Unwillingness to accept a past or present reality.

When you don't accept the truth or reality of the person being gone, out your life, you become frustrated and angry because your heart knows it is missing something, but your mind keeps trying to tell your heart it isn't. I will have to teach on that subject another time. Your mind, your will, and your emotion are all different parts of you.

Anger—a strong feeling of annoyance, vexation, displeasure, or hostility.

This is when your mind, your heart, and emotions are all in conflict. They're all telling your body something different. They are not in agreement. So when something isn't in agreement, we know it is in conflict, division. This is called confusion, unstableness of the person.

Bargaining—to negotiate the terms and conditions of a transaction. An agreement between parties that settles what each gives or receives in a transaction between themselves and compare contracts.

This part of grief is usually done with God. You asking him to do something for you, and you do something for him in an attempt to make you happy again. To help you find some form of peace and joy you once had. You try to bargain with God so you can survive another day without the hurt and grief of your heart.

Reasoning—the act of thinking about something in a logical sensible way.

At this time, you have gained a sense of peace and acceptance of the person being gone or the relationship was ended. So now you began to plan future joys and what to do next with yourself to maintain a sense of peace.

Acceptance—the action of consenting to receive or undertake something offered. Embraced, approval, adoption.

This is the final stage of the grieving process acceptance. You have finally worked through the first four anywhere from one to one hundred times in order and out of order to gain a sense of acceptance and peace. Getting to the final stage of acceptance probably took you anyway from thirty days to thirty years. This process is depended upon you the individual. But like I said in the beginning, there is no time frame for this process. Some people never complete the process; therefore, they never heal from the hurt or pain of heartbreak.

My father died in February 2002. I didn't totally accept his death until 2007. It wasn't until God sent me to work in Lake Charles, Louisiana, as a caregiver for the Sweeney family that I began to embrace the concept that my father was gone forever. Because he left me in 1998 and went to prison, so when he died in prison, I completely lose it—my mind, everything. I became very destructive and ruthless.

After one year, God really took hold of me, but I would tell myself that my father was still in prison, and he would be home soon. Well, that wasn't true at all. I was still in denial since 1998 because I never embrace the fact that he left me. I grieved him every day of my life for years. This is how I know it can take days to decades to accept someone gone out of your life. And then there was the death of my two grandmothers that still grieved me for years, the devastation of my husband abandoning us, and the death of siblings and uncles. The amount of grief in my life has been very high most of my life. And to add fuel to the fire since those family members' death, I have lost my oldest son and my mate one year apart five years ago, and I am still trying to work through that.

Then the death of my godfather, client, companion, and grandson is still fresh. One year old, so when you open the door to grief and sorrow, all of it flows out. You don't decide whose death you will deal with first. God decides that once you let Him in that part of your heart. But I have dealt with all the deaths of my past. I now truly embrace and understand how special and blessed I was to be chosen to be worthy to be in their lives. It is an honor to be chosen with the responsibility of being a caregiver. It is priceless, and you began to see the effects you have on people because of the pearls of wisdom you were given by all the people that came and went in your life. Oh yes, people teach you a lot about yourself when they exit your life. You just have to settle down, quiet down, sit back, meditate, and think about what they bought into your life or what they took out your life. People only do two things. They either add to you or subtract from you. It is your responsibility to find out who are adders to you and who are subtractors of you.

1. Passion

What is passion?

Passion—strong and barely controllable emotion. The state or capacity of being acted on by external agents or forces. The emotions as distinguished from reason. Intense, driving, or overmastering feeling or conviction. An outbreak of anger. An ardent affection. A strong liking or desire for devotion to some activity, object, or concept. An object of desire or deep interest. The sufferings of Christ between the night of the Last Supper and His death (*Merriam-Webster*).

So we see that passion is a very strong emotion, force, and desire. I became very passionate as a child to care for people, to take care of them. To stop their hurts and pains. To stop them from feeling sad, lonely, depressed, or unwanted. To stop them from being abused or rejected. But I wanted to meet their needs whatever they were. If they needed someone to talk to, I wanted to be an ear to them. A shoulder to cry on and tell them it would be okay. If they needed someone to feed them, I would; if they needed someone to watch their children, I would. If they needed help with bills, food, and clothing, I would. If they needed a ride, I would take them. If they needed their hair combed, I would do it. Whatever the need was, I always felt I was supposed to be able to fulfill it. That's why we came into contact with each other.

Even as a child, I heard someone say, "You don't just meet people to be meeting them. There are a reason and a purpose. You are supposed to find out why. You are supposed to learn something from everyone you come in contact with. You are supposed to learn something every day." So when I heard this, I took it to heart, and I never forgot it. My passion to solve people's problems are still very intense. So intense at times I can't rest until God gives me an answer and solution to the problems I have been given by people. God created me to be a thinker, be curious, an analyst, so I have always tried to find a reason behind everything.

But as I got older and wiser and began to be trained by my mentors, I learned that I was a strategist—a person with the responsibility for the formulation and implementation of a strategy. Strategist generally involves setting goals, determining actions to achieve the goals, mobilizing resources to execute the actions. My passions had taken me to places I never dreamed, before people I never imagined and gave me a very prosperous and fruitful life.

2. Purpose

What is purpose?

Purpose—the reason for which something is done or created or for which something exists.

An Intention, intent, purpose, design, aim, end, object, objective, goal mean what one intends to accomplish or attain. Intention implies little more than what one has in mind to do or bring about.

Purpose can guide life's decision, influence, behavior, shape goals, offer a sense of direction, and create meaning. For some people, a purpose is connected to vocation—meaningful, satisfying work.

For others, their purpose lies in their responsibilities to their family or friends (*Merriam-Webster*).

I have come to realize that I was created not just for one purpose but for many purposes. As I was growing up, I always had several interests and needed several different areas to express myself. I am still that way today. I carried and birthed five children, three girls and two boys. All of them are different, like different things, have different personalities. My children were given to me by God to develop my multifunctional purpose in life that He created me for. You asked how was my children a part of my purpose? God knew that I would be helping people with different personalities, backgrounds, ages, races, problems, situations, circumstances, and issues.

He knew I needed to be trained in dealing with all of this at the same. So my passion was connected to my purpose. I am one woman with many different functions or purposes. I will name a few.

I am a mother, a daughter, a sister, a friend, a companion, a caregiver, a counselor, a confidant, a mentor, a teacher, an evangelist, a wife, an aunt, a grandmother, a godmother, a CEO, a president, a lover, a fighter, a warrior, a speaker, and an author. Seem all these many roles are tied to my purpose in one vessel. We are many things to many people. We are like our Father Jehovah. Now can you see why He and Jesus have so many names? Because each time we encounter them and have experience with them, it is for different reasons, and they have to become that in which we need them for at the time as do we with people.

For example, when I am at my office Jentle Touch in Home Care where I am CEO, I can't conduct a meeting like a mother with my children. When I am at a book signing, I can't be the president of Empowerment Ministry. When I am with my grandchildren, I can't be the companion. When I am with a mentee, I can't be the wife. All these different purposes I serve requires me to perform many roles at different times in different settings that causes me to be multitalented *to fulfill my purpose with passion.*

3. Empathetic

What is empathetic?

Empathetic—showing an ability to understand and share the feelings of others. Empathy is a high degree of understanding of other people's emotions. Relating to empathy, the psychological identification with the feelings, thoughts, or attitudes of others—a sensitive, empathetic school counselor. Expressing or feeling or resulting from sympathy or compassion or friendly fellow feelings—disposed toward. (*Merriam-Webster*).

I think it is safe to say I began developing empathy as a child. I could just look at people a knew how they were feeling without them saying a word most of the time. I would be in a room full of people, and I am drawn to the person that has some type of hurt, pain, distress, or anguish in their life. As I began to be trained for the Five Fold Ministry, I learned that this wasn't just a form of empathy I had for people but rather a spiritual gift. One of the nine gifts of the Holy Spirit was given to me called the discernment of spirits. Discerning of spirits is one of the least understood spiritual gifts in the body of Christ. I strongly believe that everyone can (and needs to) operate powerfully and effectively in that gift to wage spiritual warfare effectively.

Simply put discerning of spirits means to spiritually see and understand what the Holy Spirit and demonic spirits are doing as they impact our earthly realm. It is one of the spiritual gifts Apostle Paul talked about in 1 Corinthians 12:10 (KJV). It is important to understand that discerning is not judging. Discerning or having the mind of Christ for a person or situation involves firstly operating in love. We perceive the Holy Spirit is saying/doing, but that can only be done well if we have the heart of Christ (Don Ibbitson). So when I am around people, I am always discerning different things about them, not trying to it is just a part of my makeup, mixed with my purpose and passion for the hurting the dying and the brokenhearted fueled by the love of Christ in my heart.

4.   Dedication

What is dedication?

Dedication—the willingness to give a lot of time and energy to something because it is important.

Complete devotion and faith in someone or something, like dedication to your family, a ceremony in which something is officially named. The quality of being dedicated or committed to a task or purpose. Hard work and effort that someone puts into a particular activity because they care about it a lot (*Merriam-Webster*).

When I truly learned to be dedicated to something or someone was when I was twenty-three years old. I was five months pregnant with my fifth and last child. I was living in a Battled Women's shelter, and I needed a job to get me another house. I was told about this restaurant hiring.

The restaurant name was Uncle Johnny's owned by a Greek man named Johnni Yannis. Oh, how I learned to love Uncle Johnny. But I applied for the job as a waitress. He interviewed me that same hour and hired me. Oh my god, I was so grateful because I was like, "Lord, I need a job." Let me tell you something, people. When you need a job, you will take any job available to you. I hear people say all the time, "I need a job, *but* I ain't working here or working there." *That's pride* in you talking.

That's why you're still broke, still living on government assistance, still living with family and friends, still sleeping with men to pay your bills because of your refusal to humble yourself, and this goes for men too. I see more unemployed, broke men than women. They refuse to work and find a silly woman—the Bible calls them silly women that allow men to come to live with them and layup over their children. You're feeding them your children's food with the food stamps you get for from the government, and you're giving them the time your children need to help them with homework.

You housing them while the government houses you. I have seen this same thing time and time again with men and women, and it is one of the things that boils my blood. To see a mother take from her children and give to a man, a sorry man at that. Especially if he isn't your husband, and he's not providing for your family. Oh, I can feel your temperatures rising, who does she think she is?

I am Antonette that's who I am. It is beyond a sad situation when this happens. You're getting up every day going to work, and he is still in the bed; you're getting up going to work, gotta come home and cook for him and the children that's not his, you're going to work, and he playing video games all day that belongs to your son. I have seen it all, and it all makes me sick to my stomach because a woman should never want a man in her life that bad at the cost. That cost too much to destroy your self-respect, the image in your children's eyes, and the brokenness of their spirit when you choose yourself over them. Because, women, it isn't about the man; it is about your choice of a man and you lacking your worth and value.

Back to me learning dedication, I guess the Lord wanted someone to hear that. But Uncle Johnni taught me to be dedicated. He named me Toni. He said, "Toni, we're family, and I treat you like my own daughter. Don't ever worry about money or anything. Just come to work, be on time, and I'll take care of you. We help each other."

I said, "Yes, sir, I understand."

But I really didn't understand at the time. Uncle Johnni allowed me to work up until one week before I delivered my son. He had the other waitress to bring out my heavy trays. This was my first job at a restaurant. During the course of my four and a half year career at Uncle Johnny's, I learned to be committed no matter what. I learned to go to work no matter what. I learned to care for my children no matter what. I learned to embrace new ideas and ways of life from this man. He was of the Greek culture, the cooks were Mexican, and the waitresses were black, white, and Spanish. We were all family.

I learned so much from all of them. Uncle Johnni was a man of his word, and I became a woman of mine. He has given me money for down payments for houses and cars, and money for childcare because I was dedicated to my family at home and my family at work. We never lacked in our personal lives while we worked for him because we honored him and valued him and his love and teaching to us. My husband used to get mad and take my car, so I couldn't get to work because he thought I was having an affair with my boss as did my mother. So my boss sat my husband down and told him some truths that if he would be the father and husband, he was supposed to be to me and our five children. He would have to give me money for cars and homes. Neither would I have to work so much but rather spend time home with my children.

He told my husband that we were family. He valued family above anything in life. He doesn't see us as his employees but as his family. He told my husband that I, Toni, was one of the best waitresses he has, and I'm dedicated to my family. There is nothing he would not do for me.

And he told my husband, "You are welcome to come to sit in here time if you're that insecure about Toni. She loves you, and she loves her children."

My husband thanked him and apologized. My husband would bring our son to the job for me to breastfeed because he refused to take a bottle at all. Every year in the month of February, Uncle Johnni gave me the entire month off to have family time with my family. He is who I sat at his feet for almost five years and *learned the art of dedication.*

5.   Dependable

What is dependable?

Dependable—trustworthy and reliable. If people can always count on you. To be consistent in your performance or behavior regardless of the role. To have confidence in him, her, or it.

A person or thing is dependable to whom (or which) one can go in full confidence that one will get the support or assistance required in time of need or in an emergency as to ask a friend to recommend a dependable physician, he is most dependable of our friends. Dependable term implying a character that is incalculable, or that is the antithesis of that which is fickle, capricious, or the like (*Merriam-Webster*).

I learned the art being *dependable* from Uncle Johnni.

6.   Patient

What is patient?

Patient—able to accept or tolerate delays, problems, or sufferings without becoming annoyed or anxious. Quiet and steady persevering or diligent, especially in detail or exactness—a patient worker.

Now this attribute can be tricky. I say that because you can be completely patient in one area and impatient and anxious in another or several areas. So throughout my life thus far, I have learned that

I am extremely patient in many areas but impatient in many other areas. This truly is one of the lifelong processes that will never end. Each day I decide rather to be patient or anxious.

7. Attentive

What is attentive?

> Attentive—paying close attention to something. Awake, alert, perceptive, acute, aware, heedful, mindful, vigilant. Observant attentive to what he is doing. Heedful of the comfort of others.
>
> Solicitous an attentive waitress. Offering attention in or as if in the role of a suitor an attentive boyfriend. (*Merriam-Webster*)

I think I have always been attentive to certain people and in certain situations. So since I am writing about my life as a caregiver, I will share a very special story with you. In 2007, after my husband left us, I worked three jobs mainly because I didn't want to sleep. But after months of depriving myself and neglecting myself of proper rest and food, I was forced to face reality.

This body will shut down on you when you abuse it. So mine gave me several warnings that I ignored them all. But after I was made to listen my entire outlook on life changed. I finally took an offer for a job as a caregiver, traveling to parts of Mississippi and the whole of Louisiana. I would work seven days straight and be off seven days straight with great pay. My first job was in Lake Charles, Louisiana, with the late Merritt and Ella Sweeney. Both were in their nineties. She was ninety-two, and he was ninety-three. She was bedbound, and he was mobile. They had been married for seventy years. This was the first thing that amazed me about this couple.

I asked him, "How did y'all make it to seventy years of marriage?"

He was very verbal; she was quiet. He said, "Love, respect, and hard work."

I said, "Really?"

But each day, he arose, and he would go straight to her bedside, kiss her, and talk to her, made sure he put her a fresh rose or flower out the backyard on her table, bath her, fed her, and talked to her whether she talked back or not.

He talked to her and kissed her all day every day. He continued in the same routine they had for years. Newspaper in the morning, breakfast and TV shows. He read his medical book every day because he wanted to become a doctor at first to help his brother, but he got married, and she became pregnant, so he worked for the oil refinery until he retired. He would read aloud to me each morning as she took her morning nap. I watched him love her despite her condition. I had never seen a man stand by a woman in that capacity nor care with respect. This couple changed my life and my perspective toward marriage, love, and respect. This is where I learned to be attentive in all things, not just some things.

8.   Teachable

What is teachable?

Teachable is when you are capable of being taught, apt and willing to learn. Favorable of learning.

I have always lived by the rule of the three Ls—look, listen, and learn. But in order to live by that rule, you can't think you do it all or know everything. You are supposed to learn something new every day because it is a new day that you have never seen before and a day you will never see again. So embrace the day with a set of open eyes. I told you in past chapters that you learn from everyone you come in contact with. I also say you must have a teachable spirit.

This has been my daily prayer for years. I always ask the Lord to keep me in a position that I would always need Him and greater position that I will always learn and ask questions. He has granted my prayers for over thirty years now. I am one that is always apt to learn something new.

9.   Self-Care

What is self-care?

Self-care—the practice of taking action to preserve or improve one's own health. The practice of taking an active role in protecting one's own well-being and happiness, in particular, during periods of stress (*Webster*). I continually have to tell myself to take care of me first because if I don't take care of me, I can't effectively take care of anyone else. All my life I have tried to master this one characteristic or attribute. I find it sometimes difficult because I have some many goals and deadlines that I set for myself to achieve. And many times my goals and deadlines has caused me to neglect my health, sleeping, eating, and time for myself.

I am not as bad about it as I used to be, and when I get off track, I get a strong nag. When I ignore the warnings, it is bad for me, and I usually pay a high price with my body. This is a daily decision I make to care for myself. I take me a nap every day. If I miss my nap, I am too tired to sleep at night. I made myself start taking naps to rest my mind over fifteen or sixteen years ago. I started to take fifteen-minute power naps to help me through the day. Because as a recovered addict, they tell you not to get too tired or make important decisions when you tired because your thinking and judgment is off. If you become too tired, you will want to use drugs as a pick me up or to lay you down; either way is not good for you.

So I try to practice this rule, and I think I have mastered the naps scenario because I still take two-to-three-hour naps for years. My children laugh at me when I say, "It's my nap time. I got to rest my mind." And especially when I am staying at their house. They all say I snore and talk in my sleep.

I say to them, "I don't know because I am asleep, LOL."

I take baths to rest and relax me. I love bubble baths with music playing and my time of prayer as well in the tub. Now I have done this method of self-care since I was a child and continue to this day. The point is to take care of you, love you, take you out to eat, take you a nap, take you a walk, take you somewhere for fun and enjoyment, and do something that brings you pleasure and joy. Make yourself happy, and you will guarantee two things that you did something just for you, and you bought yourself joy in the process.

CHAPTER 8

MY GIFT MADE ROOM FOR ME

A man's gift maketh room for him, and bringeth
him before great men.

—Proverbs 18:16, KJV

I have been very blessed and fortunate to be able to sit at the feet
of the greatest. Great men and woman that has taught me so
many life lessons directly or indirectly. I have had the pleasure
of caring for some of the most prominent people or their loved ones.
I will just name the arena of which these people range in and their
careers or job titles. These are the realms in which I gleaned from
them for a short time but still use my pearls of wisdom today. These
precious people had a great impact on my life.

1. I sat at the feet of a restaurant owner for four and a half
   years.
2. I sat at the feet of man that founded an organization for
   babies with clubfoot for ten months.
3. I sat at the feet of him and his wife and learned many lessons on marriage.

4. I sat at the feet of a billion-dollar real estate owner. This man owned 80 percent of the city from house to apartments to building for offices. Self-made he said.
5. I sat at the feet of a retired ophthalmologist whose grandson was a professional baseball player. That I had the opportunity to meet his wife and children. Exactly babysat the children for three days but sat at the grandparent's feet for thirteen months.
6. I sat at the feet of a beef, cow farm owner and wife. I had the pleasure of learning the lesson what was I made of. Was I sure caregiving was the career for me? See all the people feet you sit at isn't to teach to good things but rather help you see yourself and true intentions.
   I sat at his and his wife's feet for eighteen months.
7. I sat at the feet of world-famous chef parents. I had the opportunity to care for his parents until his mom passed. I spoke to him on the phone several times. His mother was the one to teach him to cook.
8. I sat at the feet of riverboat captains for nine years. Amazing men. I learned many life lessons from him and his wife. From parenting to children, to grandchildren, to marriage, to finances.
9. I sat at the feet of real estate owner that was a widow woman. I learned a sure lesson that widow women clients are far, far, far different and challenging than men widow clients. I have had the opportunity to sit at the feet of several widows, and they all have tested me in ways the men I cared never thought of during. If you want a run for your money, just care for a widow woman. But I learned to be a submissive wife. This woman allowed her husband to have full control of their lives. They moved to another country with their children to support her husband and his dreams. The house she now lives in she would tell me daily, "This is my husband's house, not mine. He wanted to live out here, not me."

She said, "I was a city girl. But he just loved this property, so I told him if he allowed decorating the house my way, I would move." And he agreed to allow her to decorate the home, and they bought and designed his dream home.

So I learned from her that you must compromise in your marriage if your husband is taking care of you and your children, what difference does it makes where you live? He's the head of the house.

I sat at her feet for over two years. She is who I have patterned my future behavior to be toward my husband. He shall have my full support of his dreams and add me to his vision. I am totally empty and available to him. But you will read about that in volume 5 *Made for Him: God Uniquely Made Me for My Husband, very powerful book if I might say so myself.*

CHAPTER 9

My Rewards, Rare Moments, and Miracle

But without faith it is impossible to please him: for he that cometh to God must believe that he is, and that he is a rewarder of them that diligently seek him.

—Hebrews 11:6, KJV

I used this scripture for this last chapter because many don't understand the richness and revelation behind this scripture. But they quote the first part all the time, "But without faith, it is impossible to please him: for he that cometh to God must believe that he is," and they stop right there and don't get the promise of the scripture. Because if you do part one and two, then what does God do for you doing your part? Part three of this scripture says he is a rewarder of them that diligently seek him. It did not say them that seek him; it says them that diligently seek him. Meaning, you are earnestly seeking him, looking for him, and God rewards you for seeking him. So here are a few of the outward reward that I received from believing and doing all of Hebrews 11:6 scripture.

Rewards

> Lo, children are a heritage of the Lord: and the
> fruit of the womb is his reward.
>
> —Psalms 127:3, KJV

My womb was blessed to carry and birth five children as a reward from God. All my children are grown and healthy. Some are married with children, so I am a grandmother. My children call my grandchildren the *seeds of Antonette*, LOL. I said, "Yes, Lord, they are."

When I tell you all my grandchildren looks like me, all my grandchildren look like me. My father had very strong genes, and we all look like him, and I have very strong genes, and all my children look like me. I got on my children's nerves during their pregnancies, so their children look and act like me, LOL.

Glory be to God. This is the joy of my life. Motherhood is priceless and the greatest reward to me.

> Beloved, I wish above all things that thou may-
> est prosper and be in health, even as thou soul
> prosperth.
>
> —John 1:2, KJV

This is our slogan and scripture for Jentle Touch in Home Care: "Jentle Touch in Home Care We Are His Hands."

Jentle Touch in Home Care is the very first company I started in June of 2014. After years of planning, preparation, and prayer, I started this company. Jentle Touch is named after my father, Jentle, who is the one that began my life as a caregiver. I provide twenty-four-hour care for the elderly, disabled, sick in their homes, or wherever they call home. I provide them with twenty-four-hour caregivers that live with them around the clock for seven straight days, and the other caregiver rotates for seven straight days.

I serve the two states of Mississippi and Louisiana. We do whatever we can to keep the clients in their own homes. I believe that you shouldn't have to be removed from your house because you are sick, or lose all your life long possessions to a nursing home just to receive care. If you are forced to sell or sign over your possessions to be a resident of the nursing home, then you can't fulfill the scripture that says Proverbs 13:22 (KJV), "A good man leaveth an inheritance to his children: and the wealth of the sinner is laid up for the just."

If you become sick or widowed and now have to give up your home to move into an assistant living facility, how are you leaving your children and inheritance? You can't fulfill this scripture. So my responsibility is to help people fulfill this scripture. That is the purpose of Jentle Touch in Home Care, and I have had the privilege to see this scripture fulfilled for many families at least twenty in my years of business. We are with the client when they slip from time into eternity.

My heart is filled with joy when I know that I have helped them fulfill their lifelong dream and promise to their children and grandchildren because God is a God of generations. Yes, it is hard to let them go, but when their assignment is fulfilled on this earth, that makes it much easier.

Real Antonette Come Forth "Spread Your Wings."

> Therefore if any man be in Christ, he is a new creature: old things are passed away; behold all things are become new.
> —2 Corinthians 5:17, KJV

That is our slogan and scripture for Real Antonette Come Forth company.

Real Antonette Come Forth is my second company. It is not just my book series, but my company I started in April of 2015. I knew that I would be writing many books and that one day, my book series would become a movie. *The Real Antonette Come Forth* book series is my life testimony of how I survived and defied all the odds that were stacked against me. How God has brought me through the hardest of times, and Jesus had never left me nor forsaken me, even when I was in the world of sin. When I would go before the Lord in prayer to be healed of all my hurts, pains, and heartbreak. When I would seek Him to give me a better life like I know he died for me to have this is what he told me. I had two years to deal with me. All the stuff I had held inside for my entire life. He wanted to cleanse me, heal me, deliver me. So I began the process of healing in 2010. In 2014, while in the shower, I hear these words: "The Real Antonette Come Forth."

I said, "What is that, Lord?"

As I walked back to my bedroom to get dressed, I heard, "Your book."

I was like, "I am not writing any book about my life. I have come clean with you, and we have worked through the greatest of my healing. No one needs to know."

The Lord says to me, "If you want to be completely healed and completely whole, you write this book, and I will heal you as you write."

Well, in April 2015, I began to write my story, and the Lord told me I had two years to complete this book. I said, "Okay, Lord, if I can stop one girl from having the life I had, I will tell my story."

I began to write my story. My outline was nine chapters at first, but when I got in chapter five, my book was thick. So I got an auction to turn the nine chapters into books and write the *Real Antonette Come Forth* book series. I designed all my book covers to show that I was bound like Lazarus in the Bible when Jesus called him forth from the grave he arose but was still bound with grave clothes on. Jesus commanded him to be loosed, and the grave clothes fell off. So that is how I was bound and called forth, and my grave clothes were commanded to loose me (everything that had me bound had to let me go). So each book I wrote, I was being loosed, and the grave clothes were falling off me as you see the covers of my books. But I completed writing this nine-volume book series in two and a half years. I was delayed because of a close death to me. But I finished. I had already written the outline for the second series, the five-book sequel to this one titled *Behind the Scene*. I already had the title of each book while I was writing *The Real Antonette Come Forth* series.

Just like I have the title to the first book after this five-book sequel. Once this sequel is completed, my writing will change. What I mean by that is my next books will still be based on my life, but the focus will be on my spiritual experiences. I called it *glory writing* based on *revelations, insights, spiritual experiences with the godhead.* Because my story is empty, and I am available you be used by my Master. He has already promised to take me into a deeper level of writing, so I call it *glory writing* for I will continue to be lead and guided by the Holy Spirit who is the Spirit of Truth and the writer of the Holy Scriptures.

Empowerment Ministry, "To empower people for Christ."

> But ye shall receive power, after that the Holy Ghost is come upon you:
> And ye shall be witnesses unto me both in Jerusalem, and in all Judea, and in Samaria, and unto the uttermost part of the earth.
> —Acts 1:8, KJV

This is our slogan and scripture for Empowerment Ministry.

Empowerment Ministry is my ministry that I started in April 2015. The same morning after I finished writing the outline for *The Real Antonette Come Forth* book series. Now I have been helping people with their companies and ministries for years now. I even had given people their business plans through dreams given to me by God. I had been given dreams of strategy for leaders of churches, COO of companies, and leaders in different areas. I was even helping to train many people for companies I worked for or help start. I began to receive many calls from people wanting me to help them start a company or get a church building, vans, or help with the current companies and churches. I asked the Lord like, "What in the world is going on? I don't have hours to spend on the phone with all these people about their companies or churches."

So He gives me the name Empowerment Ministry with the scripture from Acts. And He also said start a youth group for Empowerment Ministry. Now my last child had just moved out, not even two weeks ago. I was an empty nester. This is the moment I have waited my entire life—to walk into my house, and everything is in the same place I left it. You might not fully understand what I am saying. Allow me to help you. I have raised five children, three girls and two boys, and being the only parent in the home majority of the time. Children are always, always touching, moving, breaking, losing stuff that is not theirs. They ramble through everything. I was the only girl and the baby, so I had my own room and my own belongings. I hated for people to touch my stuff. I am still that way today. I am just funny like that. And for this to be my only request after raising my children, I thought I did great.

And now the Lord wants me to work with children.

"No way," I said. "Barely survived raising my children. No, sir, I cant. I am sorry," I said.

Well, he allowed me to create the itinerary for the intro to workforce and intro to a business seminar. He told me how much money to invest in the people that attended and to help with their clothing for business attire. I agreed, "Yes, Lord."

I hosted my first class; it was six classes over six weeks. That proved to be too much and too long, but you learn as you go. I started a clothes closet at my church for the people that attended the classes, and those that got jobs I gave gas money. But I went and meet with many business owners in Brookhaven and told them what I wanted to do, and since I had worked for many of them and had a history of getting people jobs, they agreed to hire anyone that came through my classes.

But the issue arose when I was teaching a class, and one business owner tried to tell me I didn't know what I was talking about as far as business registration, zoning laws, permits, licenses, etc. He basically tried to argue with me in my class.

I told him, "Excuse me, I already own two companies and eleven ministries that serve not just one state but two. I am offering you free information to take your business to new heights and expand *for free*. So you don't have to believe what I say. I have proof that I know what I am talking about and doing with my business in high demand in two states."

After that seminar, I went home, and I thought about it, and I said, "Lord, what is wrong with people? Here I am helping them for free. I cover all the cost. Each folder of information I taught out of costing me twenty-five dollars, and I let the people have them."

And the Lord kindly whispered, "Start the youth group." And He reminded me how I would only allow children to ride and go places with me my entire life. I have always been surrounded by children, and they were the joy of my life. How I would always take children with me different places to show them life and expose them to new things and cultures.

I said, "Well, if I got to deal with adults challenging me in my classes when I know I am right, then give me the children. Children think about what you think. They follow, and they don't argue with you, well, at least not with me."

So I started the Empowerment Ministry Youth Group with the children at my church and with my godchildren. He told me to use the system that I was bought up in at Bible Witness Camp, teach the children to learn scriptures to go on field trips but to get the parents involved with teaching the children. He said, "I want you to promote a relationship between the parent and the child through the Word of God to fulfill the scripture, Isaiah 11:6 (KJV) "The wolf also shall dwell with the lamb, and the leopard shall lie down with the kid; and the calf and the young lion and the fatling together; and a little child shall lead them."

Children are a heritage of the Lord, and they teach parents many lessons from Christ. So this has been my goal to this day. I created packages of Bible facts for the youth that the parents have to help the children learn in order for them to go on field trips. We travel to different states because I want to expose the children to many cultures and places that God will not be limited in using them because they are afraid to travel and leave home. We go to places that are educational as well as fun. I want them to have fun, but I want them to learn too. I take them to the Global Wildlife Center where they go on Safari tours to feed the giraffe, zebras, camels, and other roaming wildlife like deer and llamas.

The Marine Mammal Institute studies to learn about close up with dolphins, sea lions, sharks, rays, and birds. Sector6 Extreme Air Sports is a trampoline park. We have sleepovers, pizza parties. I teach them cooking and cleaning skills. I teach them etiquette classes to set the dinner table, fold napkins, sit down, and table manners. I teach them administration classes how to dress for success and conduct a job interview and business meetings, how to speak to the interviewer. I also teach them servanthood. We serve in the community, single parents, sick and shut in, cancer patients, college students, and the widows and to homeless women and children shelters in Mississippi and Louisiana. I teach youth to give away clothes, household supplies like tissue, soap, detergent, bleach, paper towels, dish liquid, floor care, toilet bowl cleaner, cleaning spray when we deliver to the houses.

For the shelters, we give each woman and child their own care package that includes toothbrushes, toothpaste, bodywash, mouthwash, shampoo, conditioner, combs, towels, coloring books, crayons, lotion, mirrors, Q-tips, bath sponges. Women and children care packages are packed by the youth groups in Mississippi and Louisiana. I think I enjoy myself more than the children and the people we are blessing. I am overjoyed when I can be a blessing to so many people. *It truly is better to give than to receive.*

I go into the shelters and teach the woman intro to workforce seminars. I cater them dinners and set the table with real linen and real glasses and plates, and I sit and dine with them and the children to show them that God loves them, I love them, and that "*You can make it*" through and out of any situation through Jesus.

I go and read my books to them and give them copies. Empowerment Ministry is truly my heartbeat. I thank God every day that he chose to give me this assignment to bless a blessing to his people, and I don't take it lightly at all. I have one opportunity to present them Jesus and show them real love that they don't have to work for or do anything for but receive. I have one chance to empower them for Christ because many times they are gone when I return weeks or months later.

Mz. Nette's Glory (Braiding Salon), "The Heart of a Woman."

But if a woman have long hair, it is a glory to her:
for her hair is given her for a covering.
—First Corinthians 11:15, KJV

This is our slogan and scripture for Mz. Nette's Glory.

Mz. Nette's Glory is my third company. In 2014, I was given the name of my braiding salon.

I have always loved to do hair but never went to cosmetology school for many reasons. But I could braid hair and did braid hair for income many times. In February 2017, I opened up Mz. Nette's Glory (Braiding Salon). I obtained my Mississippi braiding license. At first, I was going to braid four heads a month to help create more revenue for Empowerment Ministry that I fund out Jentle Touch and Real Antonette, mainly Jentle Touch. He is the Man that supports all my endeavors and lifestyle. So I maybe did four heads in three months because of Jentle Touch's high demand. I used the salon for my hairdresser to come to do my hair instead of me sitting at the salon. I said if Oprah can have a salon in her home, I can too, and I do.

But the Lord had other plans for Mz. Nette's Glory. He told me to turn it into a training school or learning center for my youth group to teach them entrepreneurship. I had a few upcoming cosmetologists in my youth group and to let them come practice in the salon. So I ordered the cosmetology kit they use for school with the mannequin head, blow-dryer, rollers, curlers, brushes, and combs. I purchased barrettes, rubber bands, clips, etc.

I told the youth, "You can do anything to the mannequin head, except cut the hair. No cutting at all."

I purchased supplies for manicures and pedicures for the youth to practice, a vanity for makeup application. The Lord wants me to train these children with life skills that will last them the rest of their lives and help them become productive adults for the kingdom of

God. I told these mothers, "I guarantee if you allow your child to be a part of Empowerment Ministry Youth Group, they will be productive adults you can be proud of. I can promise them that because God has promised me that for them, that they will be blessed to be a blessing to nations as I am."

I lead by example.

Rare Moments

Rare moments are times in my life that I encountered someone that has affected my life greatly that I never knew or met only, heard about them from other people.

The first rare moment was when I was in CNA Class at Kankakee Community College. We had completed our textbook studies and was now prepared to go to our clinical at a nursing home.

They divided the class up into three separate nursing homes that we might have the opportunity to have hands-on training without really disrupting the nursing home from its normal daily activities. So I was assigned to a nursing home and scheduled to meet my instructor for the next two weeks at this location to complete my class and wait to take my state test. So we arrive at the nursing home, and our instructor is walking us around to give us a tour of the facility. They paired us up two by two for the entire two weeks we will be training there. We were assigned to the same hallway with the same residents each day. They show us the showers, laundry, and dining room where we will be working.

When we get to the dining room, the instructor said, "Meet Dr. Downey."

I said, "Who?"

She said, "Dr. Downey is the oldest man here. He is one hundred years old."

My eyes filled with tears. I said, "OMG. He delivered me. He brought me into this world."

I walked close up to him, and I said, "Hello, Dr. Downey. My name is Antonette, and you delivered me in January 1976. I want to thank you for bringing me into this world. My mother loves you. She speaks highly of you all the time. That's why I remember your name."

He responded and said, "You are welcome, baby."

My heart was filled with so much joy because who ever ask who was the doctor that gave them life or delivered them? But my mother loved Dr. Downey. He delivered all her children. She spoke of him all my life. And when I got to the opportunity to meet the man that delivered me into this world, that was a strong confirmation to me from God that He wanted me on earth. This was by far *the greatest rare moment I have ever had*. Of course, I called my mom and told I met Dr. Downey.

She was thrilled, and she said, "I thought he had passed years ago."

I said, "No, ma'am, he is one hundred years old."

Rare Moment No. 2

Now I explained to you a few chapters back that Jentle Touch in Home Care affords me many opportunities to sit at the feet of the greatest. Well, this is one of those times. This is another great rare moment of my life. I received a texted from a man that had married into one of Jentle Touch Now clients, but I met him when I was working for another company as a caregiver, so he knew me for ten years now. He texted me because he knew about Jentle Touch, and I was a dedicated caregiver and now family to him.

He said, "My grandfather passed on Monday suddenly, and there is talk about getting a sitter for my grandmother. I know you're busy and have other clients, but could you consider coming to help us out?"

I responded, "Sorry for your loss, and yes, you are family, and family is always first. Let me know when you need me there, and I will adjust my schedule to accommodate you."

He responded, "Oh, thank you, Tutu. I'll have my mom to give you a call. It will probably be tomorrow."

I said, "Okay, look forward to seeing you and the call."

Sure enough, the mother calls and introduces herself.

I told her, "Sorry for your loss, and how can I be of assistance to you and your family?"

She began to fill me in on the details of the husband's death, no warning, no sickness, no signs, just died after getting a newspaper from outside. So the entire family was in shock, to say the least.

I said, "Woww, yes, ma'am."

She gave me a rundown of the wife that she's ninety-two years old and mobile, healthy with just minor issues. They went out to lunch or dinner every day. They were outgoing to the movies, very active. Salon and nail spas each week. She took the husband to the grocery every Thursday.

I said, "Okay, I am here for the family, not just the client." I told her, "I could come on that Monday."

She said, "All the family was leaving on Sunday."

I told her, "I had to rearrange my caregivers' shifts to cover the client I was caring for.

She said, "Okay."

I bet this lady called me ten times from Thursday, and I arrived Monday morning. I continued to tell her I will be there at 8:00 a.m. Monday morning. She was worried because the widow was refusing to allow me to come. She didn't think she needed help at all.

I told her daughter-in-law, "She just needs a companion. If you can get her to agree just to let me come, once I am in the door, I can deal with her."

She said, "Are you sure? I will be here. You can call me anytime, and I don't live far."

I said, "Trust me. Just get her to agree to let me come, and I will take it from there," because I am saying to myself that she has no idea *that I am the best in my field.*

I am not saying that to be prideful or arrogant, but I have been certified as the best in my field by many. You don't just say things like that about yourself. This is what others had begun to say about me and my work. I just have a way with people. The widow agreed to let me come. I arrived early, never be late for a job or meeting.

I came in told the widow sorry about her loss. She thanked me and said, "Have a seat. Tell me about yourself."

I told her I was a mother, and all my children were grown and live on their own. That I was Tutu, grandmother of ten, seven boys and three girls. I was single, and I was a hard worker with many endeavors at my fingertips.

She said, "Oh okay."

She wanted to know why I was single.

I said, "My husband left my children and I in 2007, and it was the best thing he could have done." I told her, "I was engaged, but my fiancé passed four years ago."

She said, "Okay, you can stay with me," and told her daughter-in-law to show me around.

She gave me a tour of the home. I wrote down her daily activities, family names, and weekly schedule to get started. I told them my schedule for my events for pastors anniversary program, book signing tours, and meeting with Empowerment Ministry Youth Group. We went to lunch, and then after lunch, she left. The widow took a nap, and I unpacked my car. When she awoke, I asked her to tell me about her husband and their life together.

She told me through the tears, and she continued to say, "I am sorry. I am not good company."

I told her the same thing for months, "You don't have anything to be sorry for. You just lost a huge part of your life. You were with your husband for fifty-eight years longer than I've been on this earth. You are supposed to grieve his loss. But be thankful that he left in peace. I know it's hard to see right now, but you would not have wanted him to suffer from sickness for years before his death."

She said, "No, he would not have wanted that."

She began to tell me that he was a retired chief of obstetrics in New Orleans after World War II was over, and the hospital closed. They went into private practice and handed me the newspaper write up on him. She talked and said how he loved his patients and everyone. How he saw the good in all people. And as I continue to read, the newspaper it said that "Dr. Stanley Sherman was the first New Orleans physician to monitor all his patients in labor and was also the first physician in New Orleans to use stress testing in pregnant women and chemical determination of fetal well-being prior to the onset of labor."

When I read that passage, my eyes watered, and my heart leaped with joy *because this was another rare moment for me*. I said to his wife, "OH MY GOD, OH MY GOD."

She said, "What? What is it?"

I said, "Your husband performed the test that saved my first baby, my first child, OH MY GOD."

I began to tell her that I was twelve when I became pregnant with my first child and thirteen when I had her. But because I was so young and pregnant, when I got five months pregnant, my body began to take over. I was still growing, so my body took all the nutrients from my baby, and she never gained another pound or grew another inch for the duration of my pregnancy. Now the doctors advised my mother to terminate my pregnancy. I refused to allow them to do so. I told them I was going to have my daughter. That's why God allowed me to become pregnant.

Well, I became pre-eclampsia or toxemia. They began to perform a stress test and nonstress test on me at six months pregnant. At seven months, I was admitted until I gave birth to my daughter that was two months later. They would put me in labor, monitor my daughter, take me out of labor. They drew fluid weekly from my embryonic sac to tell how my baby was developing. They said the baby gives off cells when kidneys, livers, and lungs and internal organs are developing. So they would test my fluids every Thursday. On Monday, Wednesday, and Friday, they performed a stress test on me.

On Tuesday and Thursday, they performed a nonstress test on me. Finally, on April 25, 1989, they induced my labor and let me deliver my baby girl. She was four pounds four ounces, completely healthy. She only had four layers of skin instead of five. They said to just keep her wrapped up, and she will be just fine. I told her that my baby would be twenty-nine years old on April 25—today was April 9.

She said, "Wow."

I said, "Okay, God, Dr. Sherman saved my baby. I am here to save his." I looked at her, and I said, "Your husband saved my baby, and God sent me to save you, His baby."

And we both cried and held hands and became friends that day. I studied her behavior and routine as with all my clients. I gave her space to grieve. I only talked when she was ready to talk. She loved to read, and so did I. She didn't watch a lot of TV, neither did I. I told her I don't own a TV. When I want to watch something, I go to the movies with my mother mostly. She loved to go out to eat, so did I. I was telling her about my book series that was completed, but I was now working on the sequel. When I told her the name of this book, it was originally titled *The Rules of Caregiving: How to Become the Best in Your Field*. She suggested that I should title it *Your Life as a Caregiver* since I have so many stories to tell.

I said, "You know what, I love it."

I e-mailed my publication coordinator and told her to change the title of this book because they were editing the final volumes of the *Real Antonette Come Forth Series* and adding this sequel to last page saying, "Coming Soon."

She made the changes, and here you have it, folks, *My Life as a Caregiver* was retitled by Joan Sherman of Kenner, Louisiana.

Thank you, Mrs. Joan, for your friendship.

Miracle

Miracle, everyone, is in need of one, but not all get the opportunity to experience a true pure miracle. Well, I have been afforded the opportunity to experience and live out a miracle to my life. This couple taught me to be real, be true to who I am always. This is an emotional writing for me, so I will not go into great details I will allow my writing of this eulogy speech for me.

This is dedicated to the late Captain Paul and Willie Mae Frolich Sr. of Gretna, Louisiana.

I had the previous of serving them both for the years of April 2008 to April 2017. I titled this eulogy "Made for Each Other" by Captain Anne Smith.

Made For Each Other

We were made for each other. From the first day we meet, you took me outside and said, "I'm a sailor, a seaman, from the top of my head to the soul of my feet. That is who I am and all I wanted to be. I don't deal with trash. I don't care if you're black, white, Spanish, or blue. Trash is trash, and I don't deal with it. I am a man if I give you my word and we shake on it. That's that, keep your word.

I replied, "Yes, sir," and we shook hands. We went back inside. You said I'm the Lord God and master of this ship. Don't you forget it. I replied, "Yes, sir." That was the beginning of our relationship. Since that day to this one, our love and need for each other increased greatly. We began to understand that we were made for each other. Others began to see we were made for each other. They didn't know the depth of our relationship, so allow me to tell them.

Mr. and Mrs. Paul Frolich Sr. was not only clients to me. Our relationship surpassed caregiver client years ago. They were chosen by God to "redefine" my concept of a family structure. They became my mother and father to guide me through this journey called life. Mrs. Willie Mae, our relationship began when you had a crying spell, and I got in bed with you to rock and cry with you. You told me I was too young to be taking care of you. I replied, "I've been taking care of people my whole life. I love it." We're good. Mrs. Willie Mae would talk to me day after day on how to be a great mother and grandmother to your children.

How to be a wife, friend, daughter, sister, aunt, and the many different roles we have to fulfill as a woman. But at the same time not to lose yourself along the way. She loved and prayed me through many rough and tough days.

Mr. Paul became the father, the guidance, companion, counselor, adviser, and friend I needed in my life. He was the man that continued to sit me down and talk to me about choosing a mate. And how valuable I was and "not to settle for no trash."

I continued to say, "I won't," and I haven't. He would say to me, "Ann, you married yet?"

I say, "No, sir. You are the closest thing I have to a husband," and we would hold hands, and he kissed me on the cheek. That really was a true statement. I told him, "You are my priority. You are my companion." You are the man that sat down to talk to all five of my children before they got their first jobs and went off to college. You told them, "Sit up straight and remain eye contact in a job interview and thank them and give them a firm handshake. When you go off to school, don't be playing around, learn what you there to learn because I didn't finish school. I wanted to work on the river, so I did. You told my sons to take care of your mother, I mean take care of your mother. That's your responsibility as a man because she is taking care of you. Your mother works hard to take care of you all. Remember what I am telling you, okay," and he shook their hands, and Mrs. Willie Mae hugged them all. He did this year after year for my children and I.

We became each other's companion, a lasting love affair. This is why I would drop everything in my life to care for Mr. Paul. He said I was his right hand all the time.

And I wasn't gonna fail him. I gave him my word, I gave Mrs. Willie Mae my word that I would see him to the end, and I pray I have served you well because in the end, "we were made for each other."

Rest in peace, Captain.

Love,
Anne

The End